SHIFT

201 Proven Insurance Marketing, Digital Lead Generation, and Free Traffic Strategies to Sell More Insurance and Financial Products and Get Your Time Back Now

JEREMIAH DESMARAIS

23-Time Award Winning Insurance Marketer
TEDx Speaker | Top 40 Marketer Under 40
Speaker | Coach | Author

Dedicated to the entire worldwide community of SHIFTers:
the hardworking men and women out there, protecting what matters
most. Your support and encouragement have served as an inspiration
to me and made this book possible. May your lives continue to inspire
others to SHIFT their thinking and build the businesses they deserve.

CONGRATULATIONS!

Dear Future Financial Marketing Genius,

By purchasing this book you have made an incredibly wise decision into the future of your success selling insurance and financial products.

I say this with all sincerity because you are in the position that I was in — and that many of my clients and friends were once in: looking for answers to growth. Specifically, how to use digital marketing to grow an insurance agency or financial practice.

And they found them in the ideas, techniques, and strategies in this book that you are now holding (or scrolling through online).

I paid millions in dollars of "mistakes" to learn what I'm going to share with you here. Out of those "mistakes" came hundreds of incredibly valuable nuggets and "AHA!" moments you're going to learn without having to through the pain that I did.

As a gesture to reward you on your journey, I invite you to join the online conversation and get complimentary videos, frameworks, templates, and bonus features on the official website for this book:

www.Theshiftnation.org
Go Here Now to Download Additional FREE Resources and Complimentary Videos, E-mail Templates, and Gifts to Help You Get the MOST from This Book — FREE!

Throughout these pages, you will meet some other like-minded people, people like:

- Annette*, a Travel-Insurance Agent Who Generated 324 Leads in Ten Days with $10,000 Commissions in Twenty-Four Hours Using a Simple One-Line E-mail (Chapter 2)

- Wilson, a Group Benefits Advisor Who Used a Simple Cold E-mail Template to Generate Over $350,000 in Commissions in Ninety Days (Chapter 6)

- Mike, a Financial Advisor Who Pre-converts People Before They Even Meet with Him after Adding These Two Simple Things to His Website (Chapter 4)
- Mark, Who Gets Life-Insurance Leads Using a Simple Two-Dollar Water Bottle Concept He Learned from Community Recruitment Efforts (Chapter 10)
- Chris, a Commercial and Personal-Lines Agent Who Wrote $1,500,000 in Premium Teaching What He Learned about Social Media (Chapter 26)
- Randy, a Health-Insurance Agent Who Generated $37,391 in FREE Traffic Using a Simple Three-Step YouTube Marketing Strategy (Chapter 27)
- Jeff, the CEO of an FMO That Grew by 611 Percent in Ninety Days Using My Automated Webinar Strategy (Chapter 28)
- Marty, a Financial Advisor Who Gets Divorced Women to Meet with Him Every Week to Review Their Financial Plans with a Clever "Lumpy Mail" Technique (Chapter 31)
- Nelson, a Retirement Planner Who Reduced His Cost per Seminar Attendee down to Just $20.19 Using a Facebook Targeting Technique, Which Is a Mind-Blowing 958 Percent Lower Than Traditional Direct Mail (Chapter 34)
- Plus many more . . .

That, plus 199 ideas, stories, tips, insights, diagrams, selling scripts, e-mail templates you can swipe and deploy immediately.

I truly believe that we found each other today because we are kindred spirits in being "Students of the Game" — the game of business and life.

It's in that spirit that, with this book in hand and the community and support of our online tribe, I welcome you to this journey and reach out my hand in friendship and support.

Let's begin the SHIFT!

P.S. If you're a visual learner like I am, some of the concepts I talk about in this book are presented in video format, with click-by-click explanations together with frameworks, diagrams, and templates. I recommend you register at www.Theshiftnation.org now so you have them when you get to that chapter.

*Some first names in this book have been changed to respect to client-mentor privilege . . . and some, because they didn't want competitors knowing from where they got their strategies!

Praise for SHIFT

Agents, Advisors, Brokers, Industry Experts, Carriers and Top Producers praise SHIFT:

"I definitely recommend this book to any independent insurance agent looking to grow their business. It's chock full of insightful guidance and practical advice."

— Chip Bacciocco, CEO, TrustedChoice.com

"Jeremiah Desmarais has been helping elite brokers and advisers grow their business with digital marketing for over 15 years. He thoughtfully guides producers past jargon and technical distractions to focus on the **best ways to reach great clients in today's digital world**."

— Deborah Sternberg, President and Owner,
Starmount Life Insurance Company & AlwaysCare Benefits

"SHIFT is **a refreshing departure from anything previously published on marketing, lead generation, and sales in the insurance vertical.** Jeremiah's use of current websites, techniques, and templates allow the even the casual reader to make an immediate impact on his or her business. I would challenge anyone in the insurance space not to find tremendous value in what is presented here."

— Michael Mahoney, Senior Vice President Marketing,
GoHealth.com

"I would highly recommend Jeremiah's book to any of my insurance agency clients that are looking to shift their agency's growth into high gear with this treasure trove of lots of the latest and greatest Internet marketing ideas out there."

— Troy Wilson, CEO - AgedLeadStore.com

"**Every professional who sells insurance NEEDS to read this book.** It is full of some of the best marketing techniques I've ever seen. The status quo doesn't work any more. Shift your way of thinking. Read this book, adopt its ideas and see your clients and income increase exponentially."

— Martin Caar, Editor, Health Insurance Underwriter Magazine, Vice President of Communications, National Association of Health Underwriters

"Jeremiah Desmarais is a smart thinker, a deft teacher and a genius when it comes to marketing insurance in today's digital world. Shift is a **fresh, fascinating and practical book** that shows what's possible in today's insurance world."

— Nelson L. Griswold, Bottom Line Solutions, Inc.,
InsuranceBottomLine.com

"Jeremiah never disappoints, he is insightful and entertaining and most importantly, passionate about the success of others. In fact, Jeremiah's book is so full of useful insight into building your business that it leaves you without excuses, you will be more successful after having read this and applied its strategies."

— Rob Liano, Best Selling Author,
www.RobLiano.com

"I am **in awe of the actual resources provided** to implement plans of success in SHIFT. Appropriately titled this is a **powerhouse of step by step instructions** to succeed at marketing in a dramatically changing industry!"

— Dawn McFarland, President, M & M Benefit Solutions Insurance Services, 2016 President Los Angeles Association of Health Underwriters LAAHU

"Jeremiah is one of the rare **few marketing geniuses in the financial industry** that really gets how to integrate online and offline marketing together for maximum impact. Jeremiah's mentorship and coaching helped us experience massive breakthroughs in our business and personal lives. If you are sick and tired of the same old sales and marketing ideas being perpetuated in the financial services industry, then this book is an absolute must read. Finally, someone has gathered hundreds of **the best MODERN MARKETING ideas in one single book!**"

— Jovan Will & Fernando Godinez, Advisor Internet Marketing, LLC

"There are few books in the insurance industry that are **destined to change the game** - this is one of them. Jeremiah clearly and simply lays out strategy after strategy to succeed on the front lines."

— Rick Lindquist, CEO Zane Benefits,
Co-author The End of Employer-Provided Health Insurance.

"For agents navigating the new world of sales Jeremiah Desmarais provides an indispensable map. Not only does Shift deliver much needed strategies and insights, this book provides the how-to instructions needed to implement them."

— Alan Katz, past president, National Association of Health Underwriters
www.AlanKatz.com

"Many of the fundamental values and ideas we operate by are embodied inside SHIFT. By utilizing this process organizations, advisors and teams will be able to set and achieve extraordinary results. Financial firms will create breakthroughs if they apply the principles in this book!"

— David Callanan, Co-Founder, Advisors Excel

"If you're serious about growing your business in quantum leaps, this book is one tool you can't do without. Jeremiah has **blown the lid off of financial services marketing** as you know it in his new book "SHIFT"! He's taken proven strategies that million dollar businesses use to increase their revenue and adapted them to work in your industry so you can do the same. All you have to do is follow the blueprint that he's laid out for you, step by step. Get ready for a SHIFT in your mindset, a SHIFT in your marketing activities and a SHIFT in your business."

— Aprille Trupiano, CEO, AT International, LC
www.ATInternationalLC.com

"Having been on the front lines of publishing for two decades - many books have come across my desk. This one is **a keeper.**"

— Laura Fallbach, Publisher, 401k Specialist Magazine

"SHIFT is **THE internet marketing book for 21st century financial advisors**. Learn how to prosper with on-line and social media marketing."

— Steve Moeller, Author, EffortlLess Marketing
for Financial Advisors

"Jeremiah's book is **a must read for all insurance professionals.** It is filled with action focused information."

— Billy R. Williams, PhD, Author, President
- Inspire a Nation Business Mentoring

"Jeremiah's SHIFT is a **no-nonsense guide to marketing and lead generation** that's practical and useful for not just insurance agents, but anybody looking to lock down customers and clients."

— Ben Parr, Forbes Top 30 Under 30,
Former Editor-At-Large Mashable, Author of Captivology

"A **hands-on guide to winning in the digital marketing game** for insurance agents… Desmarais provides a sound blueprint for identifying opportunities in low cost, high return online marketing."

— Bill Daniel, CEO, All Web Leads, Inc.

"SHIFT is a **generous GIFT to the insurance and financial industry**. Jeremiah could add several zeroes to the end of the price of this book, and it still would be a bargain at that price."

— Michael Levin, New York Times Best Selling Author,
AdvisorGhost.com

"**Brilliant. Expansive**. Easy to implement. Jeremiah has succeeded where no one has. To bring a shining light to the importance of digital marketing for insurance agents and financial advisors."

— Daven Michaels, New York Times Best -Selling Author
of Outsource Smart

"From the moment you open this book, it speaks volumes. What a great structure (I love the quotes and tips at the beginning of each chapter) and there are so many ideas to consider, that it really does SHIFT your thinking. Shift is a **fresh, fascinating and practical** book that shows what's possible in today's insurance world and is a must-read for anyone in the insurance business."

— Geri McHam, President, The Estate Planning Source

"Simple to follow and incredibly effective. This **industry changing book will revolutionize marketing and lead generation** while promoting growth and successful digital strategy to insurance agents and agencies."

— Ashleigh Rothhammer, VP, Sales, QuoteShark

"Jeremiah Desmarais is a genius - and agents and advisors would be mad not follow his **smart and stellar advice on digital marketing**. Read this book!"

— Amy McIlwain, Author, Global Industry Principal
for Financial Services at Hootsuite

"Shift is a **fresh, fascinating and practical** book that shows what's possible in today's insurance world. Jeremiah's perspectives, strategies, and tactics are cutting edge and should be considered by anyone wishing to grow their business."

— Bill Cates, CSP, CPAE – Author of Get More Referrals Now and Beyond Referrals
www.ReferralCoach.com

"Jeremiah Desmarais has **struck gold**. "Shift" is filled with every single proven strategy you need to know to travel down a "Massively Rewarding and Unexpected Path" to financial success. **I have never read a book that hits the mark like "Shift"** and it is must reading for every financial professional who wants to dramatically elevate his/her success!"

— Jack N. Singer, Ph.D. President & CEO, AdvisingtheAdvisors.com. Author:
"The Financial Advisor's Ultimate Stress Mastery Guide"

"Jeremiah is amazing when it comes to how to use the internet to market insurance. I've been coming to him for years with problems that this book solves. **I can't believe how much he's giving away**. Pick it up, and make the SHIFT."
— Scott Lingle, RHU, Co-Founder Remodel Health, www.remodelhealth.com

"Brilliant! This book gives away the most **powerful tools to increase your sales and marketing power by 100 fold**. A gift to the industry."
— Tom Hegna, Economist, Best Selling Author 'Paychecks and Playchecks: Retirement Solutions for Life' TomHegna.com

"Unseating the incumbent is my specialty. But HOW to get in front of the decision maker to make that case is found in the generous ideas in this book. **Read it and prosper!**"
— Randy Schwantz, best-selling author, The Wedge. The Wedge.net

"This book had me **sold from the very first chapter**. Desmarais teaches, as I do, that the key to success is giving—and for the rest of the book he gives in a big way. The 201 on-line, email, and relationship-building strategies for growing a financial or insurance practice are presented along with tested resources, so there's no way you can say "I don't know how to do this." For each strategy, the author highlights whether the strategy better serves the B2B market or the B2C market, the level of difficulty, the amount of time required and the cost. And many of the simple strategies are brilliant and virtually unknown to the majority of financial advisors I've worked with. I will be recommending this book to every advisor I know and it will be required **reading for attendees of my programs**."
— Sandy Schussel, The "More Clients" Coach www.sandyschussel.com

"**Totally blown away with the amount of practical and useful content** he shared in such a short period of time. I'm not even halfway through 'Shift' and I've already uncovered multiple fresh ideas that I can't wait to implement!"
— Eric Silverman, Owner, Silverman Benefits Group #1 of 30 Benefit Pros to Follow on Twitter, "Rising Star in Advising" - Employee Benefit Adviser Magazine as a 2015 Monthly Commentator in Employee Benefit Adviser Magazine

"This book is definitely a must-read! **Just one of the great ideas**, which we implemented in about 15 minutes, **netted our agency $249,000 in commissions**. No kidding! Brilliant."
— Lynne L. Wallace, CPCU, President, VANTREO Insurance Brokerage. Founder, National Directory of Insurance

"Everyone knows "that guy" but if you don't know THIS "that guy" you should. Jeremiah Desmarais is the **insurance marketing guru that will inspire you to take your practice to the next level** and Shift is your handbook to get to places you didn't know were possible!"

— Susan L. Combs, Past National President of Women in Insurance & Financial Services (WIFS); New York Business Journal – Women of Influence 2016; Advisor Today - 4 Under 40 2015; Insurance Business America - Elite Women in Insurance 2015 & 2016

"Jeremiah's book is the definitive source of proven business development ideas for today's financial sales professionals. No matter what type of products you sell or who your target market is, **you will find at least 10 to 20 practical ways to consistently generate qualified leads**."

— Dan Vinal, CEO Webprez

"**A portable University** of the front-line strategies working right now for insurance advisors."

— Adam Maggio, #8 Producer at AFLAC

"Jeremiah is the real deal. Having trained tens of thousands of agents myself, I know GOLD when I see it, and **this is platinum**. Ability is much different than action. I applaud Jeremiah for not only promoting positive change but for putting it all down in this amazing book. No more excuses; time to read, react & implement. One SHIFT at a time…Thank you Jeremiah!"

— J.R. Jordan, COO of reTXT, Inc & the Senior Vice President of Colorado Bankers Services

"This book reveals **unique, powerful, and field-tested techniques** that can guarantee your success in marketing to consumers the way they WANT to learn about your products: ONLINE."

— Brandon Hardy, Chief Operating Officer, Pinnacle Plus Financial www.pplusadvisors.com

"Jeremiah has **poured his heart and soul into this book** and has shared his tested and proven marketing secrets that he has compiled over the last 25 years make this book a **must read for anyone in the insurance or financial services world**."

— Gordon Quinton, Top Producer, President, Renegade Niche Marketing Systems

"SHIFT is like getting the **keys to a treasure box of ideas, techniques and fascinating insights** into the world of digital insurance marketing. Grab it!"

— Mark Rosenthal, Top Producer,
Rosenthalfiles.com

"If you're serious about growing your financial firm, but hate marketing or selling, Jeremiah's new book will give you **proven strategies for painlessly increasing your book of business**. There's a wide variety of unique and inspiring strategies to choose from that you will actually enjoy implementing and that will make you stand out to the very clients you want to attract the most."

— Maria Marsala, Strategic Business Coach to RIAs

"You can't meet Jeremiah, and listen to his words, without being inspired to take action and raise your marketing game. This book will give you the **strategies to create marketing success in your agency**, no matter how big or small."

— Clint Jones, CEO GoHealth.com

"I've learned a lot of **relevant, actionable information** that will help me take my career to the next level!"

— Cal Durland, CPCU, Advocate for the Initiative at Insurance Digital Revolution,
Past ACORD - Director of Industry Relations

"Packed with examples, direction and methods to increase the bottom line and get the ROI from your marketing that you've dreamed of. This is **THE marketing instruction manual you've been looking for**. There aren't many books that I recommend you own a physical copy of, but this most certainly is one of them. You'll find yourself referencing it for many years to come. Thanks, Jeremiah, for one of the most **useful books for the modern era of digital marketing!**"

— Tom Carolan, Award-Winning Insurance Lead Generation Expert,
www.digitalmarketmedia.com,

"Jeremiah Desmarais never ceases to astonish me (and the industry) with his ability to create and compile so many practical and powerful strategies and tactics designed to help advisors shift their practices into an accelerated growth mode. For those advisors who get and devour SHIFT, Jeremiah has forever taken away their excuse of not being able to grow their practice. SHIFT serves as both **a blueprint for growth and success as well as a easy-to-use reference guide that should be accessed time and time again**. The comprehensive nature of the information combined very actionable detail makes SHIFT a must-have for any serious advisor."

— Scott Cantrell, Agency Growth Mastermind Network,
www.21stCenturyAgency.com

"Jeremiah's brilliant insights in this book will change the way agents do business and is a **game changer** for anyone willing to apply them."

— John Kurath, Vice President,
Warner Pacific

"Desmarais **clear-eyed look at the front lines of marketing insurance** products does all of us a service in moving the industry forward."

— Dan Mangus, National Sales Director,
Senior Market Specialists

Table of Contents

Table of Contents

Get Ready for the SHIFT

*"We can't solve problems by using the same kind of
thinking we used when we created them."*
\- Albert Einstein

Why I Wrote This Book for You

I've had the honor of meeting, coaching and mentoring hard-working agents and advisors all over the world, just like YOU.

And I've learned that behind every professional insurance and securities license is a human being who really wants to make a difference.

You, my friend, are on the front lines every single day, giving people protection from the darkest moments they might experience:

- An accident that incurs tens of thousands of dollars in medical fees that they can't afford
- The death of a loved one who leaves behind mountains of debt and no insurance
- A stock market "correction" that decimates decades of penny-pinching for a couple nearing retirement
- A lawsuit from an employee injured on the job that could leave a company bankrupt
- A natural disaster that floods an office, leaving a company unable to do business
- A family car that is totaled in a hit-and-run
- A hardworking father diagnosed with heart disease
- A factory worker who injures his back on the job and can't pay his bills
- A senior citizen on a fixed income who can't afford her medication

The list goes on and on.

And there you are, in these moments of darkness, ready to provide comfort as well as financial assistance.

It may seem superficial, but when you face economic hardship, it's a huge relief to have somebody there to help foot the bill and protect what matters most.

When I reflected on all the people just like you out there, I knew I wanted to give you the tools you need to do your job faster, better, and smarter.

Together, we can give more people peace of mind.

Making the SHIFT from "Marketing Dinosaur" to "Marketing Dynamo"

It's hard, though, to perform your noble duty using outdated information and the platitudes that people pitch as gospel.

You know what I'm talking about.

"Make a good list and keep calling it."

"Ask for referrals."

"You should use social media."

UGH . . . you've got to be KIDDING me!!

No wonder so many well-meaning men and women are leaving the insurance industry. If this is what passes for valuable wisdom, I'm surprised people don't quit sooner.

That's why I've written this book.

To give you the most relevant, up-to-date "what's working now" techniques to help you grow your agency or financial practice right NOW.

Nothing here is rehashed; nothing has been recycled from twenty years ago. These are just the best, swipe-and-deploy strategies and techniques you can use immediately to grow the business of your dreams.

I go into detail about many of them on my site www.Theshiftnation.org. You can go there now to get free videos, scripts, e-mail templates, and bonuses that come with this book.

A *SHIFT* Many Years in the Making

Fifteen years ago, we saw the beginning of the SHIFT in the insurance and financial services arena when I started generating insurance leads over the Internet using nothing more than a simple landing page and paying 10¢ a click on Yahoo. (How I wish it were as easy today!)

And today, we're seeing the flames that were kindled over a decade ago.

Around the year 2000, it was rare to hear of any agent meeting with people over the phone to close business. Connecting with clients over the Internet was virtually unheard of. We did everything at kitchen tables, around living room chairs, in coffee shops, in our offices.

Internet leads were novel.

The idea of running complicated financial formulas from a device that weighs less than half a pound and is thinner than a quarter of an inch sounded like nonsense (the iPad).

We proudly presented our quotes, projections, and formulas in acetate-bound presentation folders.

Being able to show your computer screen to a person hundreds of miles away was a fantasy.

Yet, today, we do these things without thinking.

At the turn of the millennium, I was part of a six-person company providing insurance quotes to five insurance agents.

That company became a forerunner among Internet lead companies, generating 250,000 consumer insurance quote requests every single month.

Over time, I've seen the SHIFT in the way consumers want to buy insurance and financial products.

Unfortunately, brokers are still reluctant to adapt to that SHIFT.

But, I'm Thrilled to Say ... The Tide Is Turning!

More and more frequently, if you listen carefully, you hear of agents and advisors doing incredible things that we used to think were impossible.

Advisors are switching from group seminars to one-on-one screen-sharing webinars. Young agents are coming out of nowhere and growing multimillion-dollar agencies in a few years, using nothing but the Internet. (I'll share many of their stories in this book.) LinkedIn has become a hub for the highest-net-worth prospects you can find.

Facebook is turning into a hunting ground for ideal prospects, for pennies on the dollar.

The purpose of this book is to give you my best collection of tools, thinking patterns, strategies, tactics, and step-by-step guides to help you make the SHIFT to a high-growth insurance agency or financial practice.

OK, So What Is a *SHIFT*?

In Chicago, we have these massive train systems. Everybody gets around on the train or "L" — short for "elevated" — that runs throughout the city.

If you ever look down at the tracks, you'll notice a series of switches that send the trains in different directions depending on their route.

As you ride along and the train *SHIFT*s a bit here and there, it doesn't seem to be deviating much. But if you stay on the train for one mile, five miles, ten miles . . . inevitably, it ends up going in a completely different direction than when it started out.

That train isn't using any more energy than it would have if it had stayed on its original course.

But one *SHIFT* might take you to O'Hare Airport in the far northwest corner of the city, while another *SHIFT* might take you deep into the South Side of Chicago, the birthplace of blues.

The two paths couldn't be more different.

How to Set Your Business on a Massively Rewarding and Unexpected Path

As you hold this book and prepare to turn the page, you, yourself, are standing at a crossroads of a *SHIFT*.

What you do with the information in this book could put your business on a trajectory to affect dozens, hundreds, thousands, or millions more people than you are doing right now . . . and affect yourself greatly in the process.

Or it could do absolutely nothing for them or for you.

The choice is yours, my friend.

Let's do this together . . . right now.

Onward.

Whom Is This Book For?

Which type of insurance agent or financial services professional is this book for?

Those involved in life insurance, health insurance, commercial lines, annuities, retirement planning, limited death benefits, group benefits, complex self-funded programs?

The answer is:

All of them.

Now, I know that's completely contrary to the way this industry typically works.

But, if you're willing to keep an open mind and just SHIFT your thinking for the next few pages, you'll see how we can all benefit from the core principles in this book.

Many Years Ago, I, Myself, SHIFTed My Thinking

When I was heavily involved in marketing health insurance programs, I felt I couldn't learn anything from advisors who were selling life insurance, P&C, commercial, annuities, etc.

But as I opened my mind and spoke with brokers who worked in totally different markets, I came to see similarities between myself and them and a thread of commonality through us all.

Even more so, going OUTSIDE the industry and importing successful strategies has led to incredible breakthroughs in my professional career and those I've had the privilege to coach.

I've dedicated the past 10 years to studying that thread.

Drawing Inspiration from Other Markets and Industries

Some of the biggest breakthroughs in history have come from industries sharing ideas.

Roll-on deodorant was inspired by a ballpoint pen.

Viagra was originally developed as a heart drug.

Think of what you might be missing out on by ignoring all the agents who operate outside of your own narrow market.

Instead of thinking of yourself as a life-insurance agent or a P&C agent or a benefits consultant, try thinking about your work this way instead:

> *You're either a business-to-business (B2B)*
> *marketer or a business-to-consumer (B2C) marketer.*

If you market to businesses, you're a B2B marketer.

If you market to individuals, you're a B2C marketer.

Each market has its own language, needs, and desires.

SHIFT Your Mind-set

I invite you now to SHIFT your thinking, to elevate it to a higher plane where you can:

- Look at industries — not verticals.
- Look at people — not products.
- Look to OTHER industries and verticals for knowledge — not what you've been selling for the last twenty years.

If you're willing to take that plunge, this book is for you.

But — and I want to be frank here — if you're not willing to open your mind and learn from other industries, study other markets, import what's been working for others and apply it to your own business, then, I'm sorry to say, this book is *not* for you.

If this is so, please write to my team at the address in the back of this book. We'll personally issue you a prompt and polite refund, no questions asked.

Whom This Is REALLY Meant For

This book is for the insurance agent or financial advisor who is doing well but wants to do *better*.

It's for the producer who's serious about getting the results he knows he deserves.

This is not a license to print money, nor is it a "get rich quick" scheme.

It's a compilation of strategies that my students and I have used to create windfalls of commissions in short periods of time, combined with real-world, "in the trenches" frameworks that are working at the highest levels of production today.

It's a blueprint for success.

What to Expect

I hope you are excited about the possibilities that this book represents. I have much more to say to you, both about the philosophies and practicalities of making this SHIFT. I believe this is the kind of book you will look back on later and think, *That book changed my life and agency forever!*

And I hope you will pass it on to others when you finish it.

To be clear, this book is not about me. It's about YOU. It's about the incredible freedom that comes with thinking without constraints and getting practical help to reach the next level. It's about how to implement a SHIFT in the way you think in a way that transforms your business — and as a result, your life — for the better.

In these pages, I will also be introducing you to other agents and advisors, who have become SHIFTers and who, today, are using digital marketing in ways they never thought possible. Many of them have been in situations that you will recognize from your own life, and what they did about their old ways of thinking will inspire you and give you ideas for embarking on your own SHIFT journey.

I want to be clear, again, though: this book is for agents and advisors who want to *work*, who know that success takes time.

If you're on your last dime and just scraping by, focus on the lowest-cost strategies first. Then, as the commissions begin to roll in, use the profits to reinvest in yourself.

If you already have a good profit base and want to grow more quickly, you can afford to be more aggressive.

And if you need additional help, you may want to check out my private coaching program or one of my mastermind groups.

Wherever you are in your career, this book provides everything you need to create new lead sources, appointments, and commissions — starting today.

These tools work for agents and advisors who sell:

- Health insurance
- Annuities
- Life insurance (whole and term)
- Senior insurance products
- Medicare and Medicaid
- Financial planning services
- Retirement planning services
- Investments
- Commercial lines

- Homes and automobiles
- Group benefits
- Defined benefits
- Limited death benefits
- Social Security benefits
- Fiduciary advice
- Real estate investment advice

If you're ready to work, then this book is for you.

How to Read This Book

I've broken "SHIFT" into three books, each one covering an area of concentration that will increase your leads, prospects, partnerships . . . and commissions.

I wrote this first book with the intention of making it the most highlighted book on your shelf.

Every Chapter Is Full of Tried-and-True Strategies

There are no high-level theories here. There's nothing you need to "test out" to make sure it works.

Each and every concept in this book has been used by *someone* and been proven to increase revenue.

Combined, the value of these ideas has generated $1.7 billion in premium.

At the beginning of each chapter, I've outlined four elements to help guide you on what to tackle depending on your time, budget, and tenacity.

Here's an example:

> Application: B2B, B2C
> Difficulty: Easy
> Time to implement: Five minutes
> Cost to implement: Free

The "Application" section will tell you what market this is ideal for. B2B is "Business to Business," e.g., commercial lines, group benefits, C-suite, 401(k) plans, etc.

B2C means "Business to Consumer," e.g., health insurance, retirement planning, personal lines, Medicare, etc.

Each chapter contains a specific, measurable, actionable tip (and sometimes, two or three).

A takeaway summary at the end of each chapter will help you implement each tip in five or fewer steps.

NOW, THIS IS IMPORTANT: MY $26 MILLION "SECRET"

Once you've found an idea you'd like to try, *put the book down and don't pick it up until you've actually tried the idea!*

I'm dead serious about this.

I did this when I was working my way through a book a few years ago written by my mentor and friend, Jay Abraham (*Getting Everything You Can out of Everything You've Got*). By following that disciplined mind-set, my team and I *generated $26 million in lifetime customer value in nine months — and I never even finished the book!*

This approach works.

As you go through the strategies and tips, you'll see results. That, in turn, will help you build momentum.

Before you're halfway through this book, your head will be swimming with ideas, but don't let them just sit there. Turn them into action.

Immediately use the strategies that speak to you.

Ignore the ones that may not be as good a fit for your market.

Just keep moving.

Let's Get Started

So grab your pen, close the door, and reach for your favorite beverage.

Let's start this journey together.

Open your mind, take a deep breath, and together, let's make that SHIFT.

CHAPTER 1

A Crash Course on Building Engagement with Digital Marketing

"There is more happiness in giving than in receiving."
—Acts 20:35

Application: B2B, B2C
Difficulty: Easy
Time to implement: Time to read this chapter,
    lifetime to apply
Cost to implement: Free

If there's one grounding philosophy in my entire body of work that will help you the most, it's the power of giving.

The greatest influencers of our time have been incredible givers. Both Gandhi and Martin Luther King Jr. were incredible humanitarians who gave of themselves for what they believed.

The Bible gave us this quotation in its original form more than two thousand years ago: "There is more happiness in giving than in receiving." It has since been reworked hundreds of times.

That's because it's based on a psychological principle that applies to every single human being in the world, including your insurance and financial prospects.

Dr. Robert Cialdini, author of the landmark book *Influence,* says humans aim to treat others as they're treated, meaning that we have an innate instinct for returning favors and paying back debts.

This is called the *theory of reciprocity.*

This theory makes us feel obligated to offer concessions or discounts to those who have extended the same to us — because we're uncomfortable when we feel indebted to someone. Have you ever had a friend that just kept giving to you? Do you remember how it felt not to give anything back?

That's the feeling we're talking about.

And engendering that feeling is one of the most powerful things you can do in marketing your products and expertise.

Here's my Giving Formula that got a standing ovation at my TEDx Talk, "The Democratization of Marketing":

Step 1 — Give first.

Step 2 — Give more.

Step 3 — Give again.

Step 4 — Ask for the sale.

To illustrate this point, last weekend I was at a high-level mastermind for high-powered insurance advisors. Each had paid $25,000 to be in that room.

I was invited as a guest speaker to this intimate group and I shared some strategies that you'll be learning in this book.

After my talk, we went on break, and, one of the advisors came up to me and introduced himself.

He said, "Jeremiah, I have learned so much from reading your e-mails and watching your videos, but have never bought anything from you. I feel like I OWE you to engage your services now. How can we make that happen?"

That's the power of giving at work.

It's funny, but this is the *exact opposite* of what usually happens in marketing.

Most agents and advisors don't give anything up front except a quote. Then they ask for the sale.

You Must Engage to Succeed

To help you SHIFT toward a reciprocity-based approach, I'd like to teach you a concept called the "Incredible Engagement Engine."

Think of it this way: the currency you and I operate in is goodwill.

If you have lots of goodwill, you will have respect, open ears, and people who are at least open to the idea of doing business with you.

On the other hand, if you're empty—if you don't provide value, if you don't educate—then your goodwill is empty as well. It's like a bank account; you can only make a withdrawal once you've made enough deposits.

In the interest of full transparency, this is what I'm hoping to do with you through the chapters of this book: I want to build a mountain of generosity between you and me.

You see, the odds are pretty high that I don't know you yet. Maybe you'd never even heard of me before picking up this book; though, believe me, I would love the opportunity to meet you, as I feel we are kindred spirits.

You may flip through this book, use some of these game-changing techniques, and never need to see me again! And I'd be completely thrilled if I heard that you had achieved success by using one or more of these principles.

But a small number of you—maybe YOU—will feel that a bond has been created between you and me as you turn the pages, and you'll want to work with me, in either my group programs or one-on-one mentoring, or you want to use our services to actually DO some of these things for you.

This will happen only AFTER I've delivered value for you. That's why I didn't cleverly disguise this book as a "secret" sales pitch to buy my programs or come to my events. Believe me, many publishers told me I should do it that way, but I vehemently refused!

There's no secret carrot I'm hiding here. I'm holding nothing back. Everything you need is here in this book—everything you need to help you grow, prosper, and earn your rank among the top performers in this business.

That brings me back to you. Most advisors today struggle with marketing because they don't know how to give value.

In the prospect's mind, the advisor who gives the most is the one who most deserves his hard-earned money.

And there's really no better way to build your engagement engine than through digital marketing.

The good news is that's it's simple, it's quick, and it requires little-to-no investment.

The Three Most Powerful Categories of Digital Marketing

So, here's your push. There are three main types of digital marketing, what I call the Digital Dominance Drivers:

1. **Inbound.** You put out great content and people find you.
2. **Social.** You share and interact via social networks, such as Facebook, LinkedIn, and Twitter.

3. **Outbound.** You use various techniques to reach your target audience and convert them into prospects by engaging them in conversation.

In our journey together through this book, I'll share with you how to develop each of these drivers by offering practical, real-world examples you can follow and start to implement right now.

This may seem contrary, but I'll start with the third driver, outbound marketing, by giving you a simple yet incredible story of one of my clients who sent out a single e-mail. The results were nothing short of earth-shattering.

CHAPTER 2

The Nine-Word E-mail That Generated 324 Leads and $8,000 in Commissions in under Twenty-Four Hours

"Simplicity is the ultimate sophistication."
—Leonardo Da Vinci

Application: B2B, B2C
Difficulty: Easy
Time to implement: Five minutes
Cost to implement: Free

According to a McKinsey study, the average worker spends thirteen hours a week — 28 percent of his office time — on e-mail. This multiplies out to (yipes!) 650 hours a year writing and sending e-mail!

This begs the question, what does it look like when you total all those words over the course of one year?

According to the personal-assistant app Cue, which is a hub for services such as contacts, calendars, and e-mail, it adds up to 41,638 words.

In 2012 Cue released some data based on a sample of its users. Though the average number of e-mail messages each user received last year was just over 5,000, the output of words sent was comparatively massive. If you put those 41,638 words in perspective, it is about the size of a 166-page novel.

So if each of us is writing a novel's worth of e-mail every year, why does it feel as if we're getting very few results from this massive effort?

The answer could be in the way we write them.

The Problem with E-mail

Most of the e-mail messages insurance agents and financial advisors write today are not only filled with terms that are difficult for the consumer to understand (PPO, HMO, co-pay, market correction, bottom-up investing, etc.). Many are WAY too long and require too much time and effort to read and digest.

Nobody wants to sit and read through a sales pitch; people want to grab little pieces of content here and there. They want people to get to the point.

But most of us were trained to write long, formal e-mail messages — the same way we used to write letters and faxes.

My suggestion to you is — wherever appropriate — use short e-mail messages.

Very short.

I'm going to give you a nine-word template for the highest-converting e-mail you'll ever send.

To date, it's generated well over $500,000 in commissions for those who have used it.

Use One Question to Start a Conversation

The technique is simple: ask ONE question of the reader. Your goal is to encourage a reply or start a dialogue. That's it.

Here's an example of a traditional e-mail (in other words, what *not* to do):

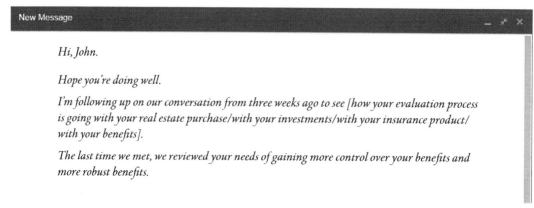

New Message

Hi, John.

Hope you're doing well.

I'm following up on our conversation from three weeks ago to see [how your evaluation process is going with your real estate purchase/with your investments/with your insurance product/with your benefits].

The last time we met, we reviewed your needs of gaining more control over your benefits and more robust benefits.

I have taken the time to review your current HMO, and explored what would happen if we integrated a TPA with a different PPO that had the co-pays your employees were looking for.

I'd love the opportunity to have a follow-up call with you and your CPA to discuss this further.

Sincerely,

John Smith
Osmond Insurance

Do you get the idea?

But if you're ready to make your first *SHIFT*, there's a much better way.

The $8,000 E-mail

One agent, Annette, tried this strategy and sent the e-mail I recommended to her list of prospects at 9:05 in the morning.

At 11:53 a.m., she texted me, "Please stop the madness. I can't keep up with the constant flow of responses!"

Then she wrote, "Crazy. More requests just came. I can't believe what a one-liner did!"

And all she did was take a very personal, one-on-one approach.

In that one day, she closed eight deals for a total of $8,000 in commissions.

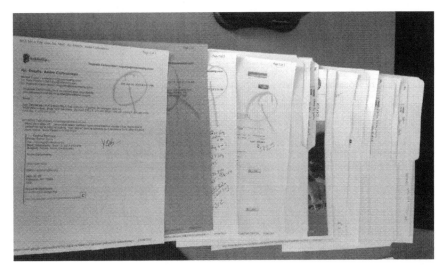

Here's a picture of the closed cases Annette won within twenty-four hours of using this e-mail. Total commissions in twenty-four hours = $8,000. After one week, it was $20,000.

Copy this e-mail template right now:

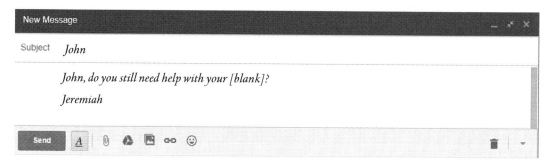

In the blank, you can put *investments, real estate, buying a home, insurance, senior insurance, Medicare, benefits* — whatever.

BAM! That's your nine-word e-mail!

Warning: Don't Change a Thing!

Send it EXACTLY as shown above.

Don't add anything underneath it or above it, other than what normally appears in the personal e-mail template you send from Outlook or Gmail!

One carrier I consulted with sent this to ten thousand people, but decided to get clever. (In other words, he didn't follow my advice to the letter.)

After the question, he wrote, "Because we've got a whole bunch of great products. We've got life insurance, we've got dental, we've got disability, we've got . . ."

And it didn't work.

Because it didn't look like it came from a human being. It looked like it came from a marketer trying to engage — and failing.

Why This E-mail Works Every Time

One commercial-lines agent had her team send my nine-word e-mail to a few B2B prospects they hadn't heard from in a while.

The same day, they got two responses that led to two meetings. Fast-forward sixty days, and those two meetings brought in $240,000 in commissions.

All from one little e-mail!

There are a lot of reasons why this nine-word e-mail works:

- It doesn't look like spam.
- It offers help rather than a product or a service.
- It's personal and implies a previous interaction.
- It's nonthreatening.
- It seems to continue a conversation already in progress.

But the number-one reason is this:

It doesn't require any effort to mentally process this e-mail.

In today's screen-obsessed society, most people don't take the time to reflect and think — but they do value brief, meaningful, personal communications.

Using tools such as MailChimp, GetResponse, AWeber, and others, you can personalize a thousand e-mail messages at once, making each one look as if it's being sent from one individual to another — and only to him.

The Takeaway 👍

☐ Send the nine-word e-mail to a list of prospects you've targeted before but who have never responded. Test the subject line "quick question" — yes, all lowercased. This converts higher, which you'll learn more about later on.

☐ Use an automated tool to personalize the name in the e-mail.

☐ Fill in the blank with the product or service you provide.

☐ Don't change anything else or add any other content.

CHAPTER 3

The Best, Most Cost-Effective Ways to Give Your Brand a Makeover— and Why Doing So Matters

"Your brand is what other people say about you when you're not in the room."
—Jeff Bezos

Application: B2B, B2C
Difficulty: Easy
Time to implement: One to four hours
Cost to implement: $29+

Let's do a quick social experiment. Look at the front cover of this book.

Do you like it?

Whatever your answer (and I hope you said *yes*), chances are you made up your mind within 1/20th of a second

First Impressions Mean More Than You Might Think

Researchers at Carleton University in Ottawa, Canada, conducted a fascinating experiment on how quickly people judge a business based on the look of its website.

First, they showed volunteers the briefest glimpse of pages that had already been rated as either easy on the eye or visually jarring. They found that study participants developed an opinion within the first *fifty milliseconds* of viewing the website.

Then, they asked them to rate the website for visual appeal on a sliding scale. Here's what was incredible: even though the participants had seen the image for just 0.05 seconds, their verdicts matched those of the folks who'd seen the page for longer!

What this means for you is that, unless you nail it with your first impression, your visitors may jump off your website before they even have a chance to learn about the value you offer.

Great Design Says More About Your Value Than Anything Else

There's also a psychological phenomenon that occurs when somebody has a positive first impression of your business card, website, brochure, or even video.

It's called the "halo effect." It means that people tend to overlook minor faults if the whole picture is pleasing. If you have a great website design, visitors will actually rate your content as being better than it is. The design creates the halo. It tells the consumer that this is a strong brand.

This is because we are all prone to cognitive bias. People love to be right — so they will continue to use a website that they decided from the outset was great, just to convince themselves that their initial decision was the right one.

Standout Design Without Breaking the Bank

So, how can you create that great first impression within a limited budget?

With some basic tools and a few hundred dollars, you can easily create the impression that you used the best design firm in the city.

Your Logo

As a former art director, I know that professional logos can run anywhere from $2,500 all the way up to $50,000 or even $100,000.

But who has that much money to drop on a logo?

Instead, there's a great website called graphicriver.com. They have forty-eight thousand logo templates, starting at $29, with styles ranging from contemporary and comical to high-end and approachable. Icons, mascots, wordmarks — the range is staggering.

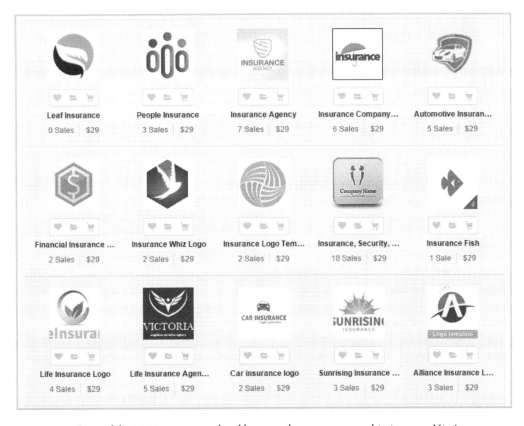

Some of the 1,382 insurance-related logo templates on www.graphicriver.com. Nice!

And if you want to make a few tweaks to one of their designs, you can have a designer work on it for just a few extra bucks. So right there, you've gotten an amazing logo for about $30.

If you've got a bit more to spend, then head over to 99designs.com.

There, for a minimum project fee of a few hundred dollars, you'll have access to hundreds of designers who will compete for your project, giving you ideas as you go.

Once you find the "perfect" one, you award him the job and get the branding you love.

Some cool logo concepts starting at $265 on www.99designs.com.

Your Business Card

Now that you have a logo, the next step is business cards.

My favorite source is moo.com. Moo specializes in higher-end and luxury business cards, stickers, and flyers. They have a gorgeous array of stationery and expert-produced design styles.

All you do is upload your logo, pick your style and stock, and you'll get your cards in about a week. I've used my Moo business cards at networking meetings with some of the top marketers in the world, and every time I hand someone my card, he says, "Wow." It's that impressive.

My personal favorites are in the extra-thick luxe range, printed on 32-point Mohawk Superfine paper.

Gorgeous business card designs start at www.moo.com.

Your Brochure

Now, let's talk about brochures.

I love Stocklayouts.com. They have some of the most beautiful designs, and the site is really easy to use. You just buy a brochure template and download in Microsoft Word format. Then, you edit the placeholder content.

And if you're looking for postcards, trifold brochures, or any kind of signage, you can buy an entire set of designs for around $200.

A financial-planning brochure template you can snag for $99 on www.stocklayouts.com.

Your Video

Let's talk about video next.

A lot of people are scared to make a video because it feels so beyond their skill set. Well, that's where VideoHive.net comes in.

Here, you can get tens of thousands of premade, stock videos to use within your own corporate or marketing videos. You'd be surprised by how many professional videos that you see on television actually incorporate videos from VideoHive.

And with selections starting at just $3, it's a no-brainer to pick a couple for the next video you produce.

Some of the selections that come up when searching for "happy senior couple" on VideoHive.

Here's an example of how we used a simple $6 VideoHive video to create a promotion.

One of my Platinum-level clients was holding a live in-person dinner seminar for retirees. I advised him to create a simple video to promote the event, which he did.

We then bought some ads on YouTube to show it to people in the same ZIP codes he was mailing to, when they were surfing YouTube. You know those annoying little videos that show up before you watch a YouTube video nowadays? That's what we showed to every person over sixty-five in his ZIP code.

After the event was over, we counted: 20 percent of attendees came from the YouTube promotion featuring that video!

A bigger breakthrough came when we found that the cost to generate an attendee online was only $20.19, compared to $226 when using postcards! I share the exact ad we used and the strategy in an upcoming chapter.

Bonus Video Tip: Doodle Videos

But what if you want to create a custom video and control everything from start to finish?

One type of video that gets consistently incredible conversions is the "doodle-explainer" video. These show a hand drawing an image, and you can't help but stick around to watch what unfolds. You can get a video like this for as little as $5 from fiverr.com.

We did an experiment and found that the doodle videos perform extremely well when used in Facebook marketing.

According to Salesforce, the telecommunications industry typically has the highest Facebook ad click-through rate, at 0.919 percent. But the doodle video we tested got a 39.2 percent click-through rate on Facebook ads! That's a ridiculous 4,266 percent increase in conversions over industry standards!

Doodle videos are powerful because they take viewers back to childhood. Do you remember the first time you saw somebody draw something on a piece of paper? Watching it has a hypnotic, mesmerizing effect that you can't pull away from.

As soon as the pen hits the paper, the loop begins. We are creatures of completion, so we want to see what's at the end of that loop.

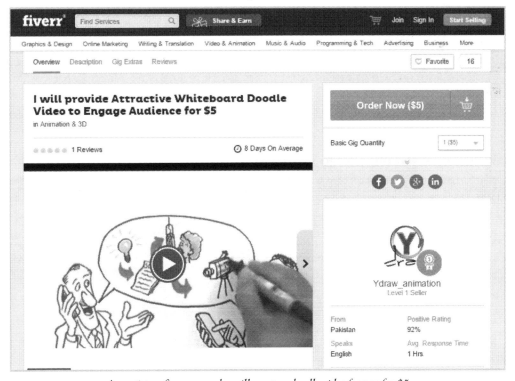

An artist on fiverr.com who will create a doodle video for you for $5.

Your Audio

Have you ever noticed that videos with background music lift you up a bit as you watch them? That's because you're not just listening to a voice or to music. You're actually hearing a heartbeat.

Studies show that videos with subtle heartbeat sounds or music with a heartbeat pace raise the blood pressure and excitement level of the person watching them.

So if you want to engage your viewers and tap into their emotions, try adding some royalty-free music to your videos.

There are tens of thousands of musicians around the world composing incredible soundtracks. These could easily be featured in movies or television shows, but they're available on a royalty-free basis for as little as $10.

One of my favorite sources for that music is pond5.com, which has an amazing, well-curated selection. Plus, you can sample everything on the website before you buy.

Another source that is really coming up in the royalty-free music world is AudioJungle.net. There, you can browse more than 268,000 royalty-free audio files that start at just $1.

Your Presentations

A simple way to upgrade your presentations instantly is with stock photography.

Two of my favorite sources for quality stock photos are PhotoDune.com and iStockphotos.com.

But . . . danger, Will Robinson, danger! Whatever you do, avoid pulling images from Google search. Many of these are copyright-protected and may have royalties tied to them, in addition to having too low of a resolution to provide a quality image.

I've heard of several insurance agents who paid professionals to build them a website, only to receive an immediate cease-and-desist notice from an attorney because that professional had lifted images from the Internet without paying for them. Ouch!

So be smart and pay for your images, or you may end up paying a ton for them later on. PhotoDune images start at just $1. iStock works on a credit system that makes the photos cost anywhere from $3 to $5.

Armed with this information, you have no excuse to bring a boring presentation into a client meeting.

So, remember: making a SHIFT involves transforming yourself from an everyday advisor to one who makes a powerful and lasting impression.

Your website, business cards, brochures, presentations, and videos should demand attention and speak to people within a split second.

And if you've already made that SHIFT, then you know how good it feels.

Summary

People are making decisions about you and your brand in less than a second. Its therefore important to have great-looking business cards, website, and collateral to help build the "halo effect" around your venture right at the moment when people are deciding whether or not they should do business with you.

A variety of online resources can provide you with an incredibly professional look for a few hundred dollars — much less than what traditional agencies charge.

The Takeaway

- ☐ Buy a premade, professional logo from graphicriver.com.

- ☐ Moo.com has great, luxurious, professional-looking business cards.

- ☐ Stocklayouts.com is an amazing source for brochure or other collateral design.

- ☐ VideoHive.com has stock footage you can use to spruce up videos. Or, you can hire a professional on fiverr.com to make a doodle-explainer video for $5.

- ☐ Pond5.com and AudioJungle.net have great, royalty-free music you can use as background in your videos.

- ☐ PhotoDune.com and iStockphotos.com offer stunning photos for as low as $1 per image.

CHAPTER 4

The Surprising Automated Trust-Building System—Using Photos

"A picture is worth a thousand words."
— Old Proverb

Application: B2B, B2C
Difficulty: Easy
Time to implement: Half a day
Cost to implement: $600+

Over time, Michael Kitces of XY Planning has noticed something wrong with most advisors' websites. Fixing it is simple but the change can make a world of difference in conversion rates.

Put a picture on your website.

It sounds incredibly simple, but it's amazing how many advisors have no photos whatsoever on their sites.

There's no way to see what they look like.

I hear a lot of advisors say things like, "Well, that doesn't matter because my business comes from referrals." But it still matters. The reality of consumer behavior these days is, "I don't care if I was referred to you. I'm still going to type your name into Google."

First, they want to make sure no stories about criminal activity come up.

Second, they're hoping to see some kind of website that validates you as a professional. They want to see *you*: someone who looks professional, who they might want to do business with.

We are social animals. We are very visual. As human beings, we crave a visual connection with people. We like to be able to see each other and interact visually.

If you look at the studies out there, you'll see that website visitors connect much more readily to visuals than a wall of text.

When I get to the bio page for most advisors, what do I see? A giant wall of text with no picture. How can they hope to connect with potential clients?

You'll never know how many million-dollar prospects who were referred to you by someone checked you out online, didn't connect, and moved on.

At a bare minimum, you need a picture up there — and not just of you. You need a picture of your staff, as well. If your clients are going to interact with people other than you, they want to know whom those individuals are. We all love to put a face to a name.

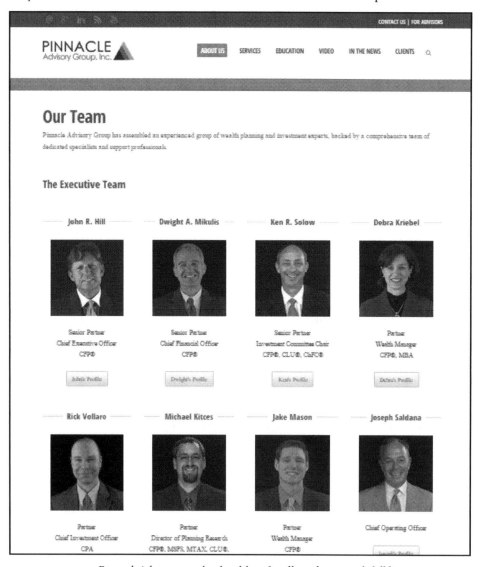

www.PinnacleAdvisory.com has headshots for all employees, with full bios.

These should be professional headshots with uniform backgrounds — not personal photos provided by your team from their family vacation, or cropped from wedding photos where you can see the other person's shoulder! You're trying to convey your professionalism in order to convince people to invest in you — sometimes large sums of money — so hire a photographer.

You can find some amazing ones on Craigslist. I once got a political photojournalist whose work has been in the *New York Times* for an entire day for just $600.

This is remarkably inexpensive, and delivers a 1,000 percent ROI once a prospect decides you're trustworthy based on your photo.

Now, take things up a notch.

A picture is the bare minimum.

The ideal is a video.

We can all relate to a picture but we relate even better to a video.

Think of all the things that normally happen in that first interview with a prospect.

They're trying to figure out if they like you, how you communicate, if they trust you, if they're connecting with you. If they don't like you, it won't go anywhere.

A video on your website introduces you to your prospects, so that first-meeting business is already done. If they book an appointment with you after seeing your video, they're very close to doing business.

And if they don't feel a connection while watching the video, they probably won't schedule a meeting — thus saving you an hour of time trying to make a deal that would never happen.

At Michael's firm, every advisor has a two- to three-minute introductory video on the website in which they say a little about who they are and why they do what they do.

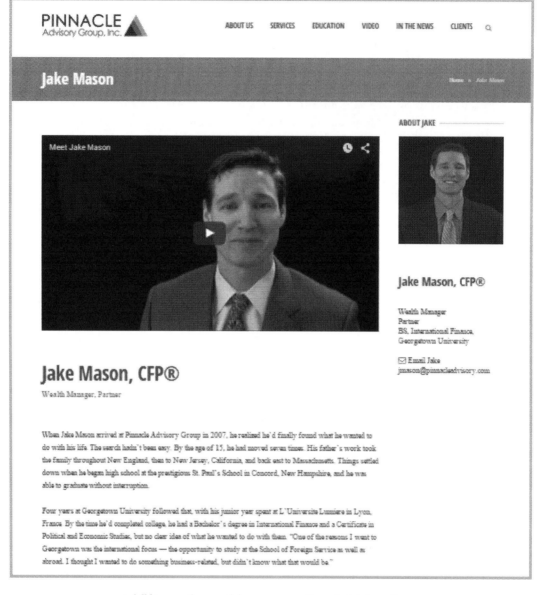

A full bio page for one of the partners at Pinnacle Advisory Group.

Quite often, they get inquiries through their website that say things like:

I was referred to your firm. Came and checked out your website, looked at all the advisor videos. Really liked Jake. Please have him contact me.

And just like that, a complete stranger has visited the website, looked around, and bonded with a specific advisor who they're now asking to do business with.

Summary

Even if you are referred to someone, chances are they will still research you online. If you have an outdated or, worse yet, NO profile picture, there's a good chance you're losing prospects.

Fortunately, this is an easy problem to fix by investing in a quality headshot for everyone on your team. You can take things a step further by recording short videos featuring each member of the company.

The Takeaway

☐ Hire a professional photographer to take a headshot of you and any staff and partners.

☐ Include the headshots, along with a brief profile, on your website.

☐ Add a two- to three-minute video for each person for maximum impact.

CHAPTER 5

One Simple Trick for Writing Great E-mail Messages

Application: B2B, B2C
Difficulty: Easy
Time to implement: Five minutes
Cost to implement: Free

In this book, I discuss e-mail marketing and writing in general quite a bit. So before we jump into the strategy of writing e-mail messages that get opened and convert, I'd like to share with you an amazing technique I know will help you.

You see, dear marketing maven in the making, writing copy or e-mail messages may be one of the most challenging tasks you'll encounter as an insurance agent or financial advisor. You may know *what* to write, but when it comes *how* to write it, you're stuck.

So, I'm going to teach you a trick for more effective copywriting that I use all the time. In fact, I'm using it right now, while writing this book.

Can you guess what it is?

Who's Your Number One Fan?

Before you write an e-mail, postcard, or direct-marketing letter — anything that will go out to a number of people — I want you to think of the one client who loves you most: your NUMBER ONE fan.

This can be a past or current client: someone who is *extremely* happy to hear from you when you call him, someone who *always* replies when you send him an e-mail. Someone who is so thankful for your knowledge and expertise when you sit down with him and share a strategy for success.

Remember how good it feels to have a client react like that?

Well, I want you to think about writing your e-mail messages to that person *only*. Do that, and you'll find your self-doubt begin to disappear.

Here's Why That "Audience of One" Is So Important

When we write an e-mail to a group of people, we often write defensively, protecting ourselves so that we don't seem unprofessional or come across as too personal or give away too much information.

But when you're connecting with someone one-on-one and helping him with a specific problem, that's when you really shine.

So why not write e-mail messages the same way?

Struggling? Here's What to Do

If you're having a hard time with this, just find a picture of your number-one fan on LinkedIn or Facebook. Print it out and put a copy of it right in front of your computer. Right at the top. You can literally just tape it there. Now, when you're writing an e-mail, look at that person and *just write it to him or her.*

You'll notice that your copy starts to flow a lot more effortlessly. You'll enjoy writing to that person. And your writing will be conversational and effective.

Summary

As we progress through this book and journey together, you may find yourself getting stuck a few times when you go to write some copy. Don't worry!

By imagining you're writing to just one person — that favorite fan of yours — you can find the unique voice that will help the words flow out of you, allowing you to write genuine copy.

The Takeaway 👍

☐ Visualize your most adoring client.

☐ Tape his picture to your computer.

☐ Write your next e-mail blast to *just that person.*

☐ Watch your copy start to flow more effortlessly.

CHAPTER 6

The Cold E-mail Marketing Template That Generated $350,000 in Commissions in Ninety Days

"New ideas are sometimes found in the most granular details of a problem where few others bother to look."
—Nate Silver

Application: B2B, B2C
Difficulty: Moderate
Time to implement: Two to four hours
Cost to implement: Free if manual, $50+
    per month for automated services

Now, I'd like to share with you an incredibly powerful template that David, an advisor out of Chicago, used to set up power partnerships with local and international businesses in a matter of days — with hardly any work on his part.

One group-benefits agent out of St. Louis used a version of it to close one deal that brought him $350,000 in commissions in less than ninety days! The industry doesn't matter, but the psychology of the approach does.

To understand WHY this template is so powerful, you have to understand that the majority of cold e-mail messages (those sent to people with whom you have no prior personal connection) are often poorly written.

So I crafted this template for David to use in combination with a LinkedIn campaign I architected. In one experiment, a version of this very same template generated eighty leads and eight appointments in twenty days from a group of LinkedIn contacts!

It was sent to people who agreed to connect on LinkedIn, and who were our *ideal* target audience. However, you can send these to *any* type of prospect with whom you're trying to get a meeting.

If you're starting from scratch and don't have many lists of connections, consider buying lists of businesses and using an e-mail service such as www.clickback.com. They specialize in helping marketers send out cold e-mail messages to businesses. Another great vendor is outreach.io to help you automate this approach.

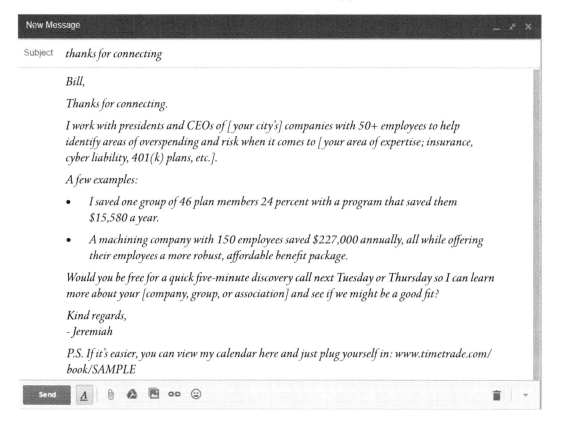

This kind of e-mail works for three reasons:

1. It's personalized to the recipient.
   I work with presidents and CEOs of [your city's] companies with 50+ employees.

2. It uses very specific data to cite the success of the offer being pitched.
   I saved one group of 46 plan members 24 percent with a program that saved them $15,580 a year.

3. It includes a direct call to action with an option to book an appointment immediately.

Would you be free for a quick five-minute discovery call next Tuesday or Thursday so I can learn more about your [company, group, or association] and see if we might be a good fit?

No one size fits all, so use this template as a starter and customize it to your specific industry, market, and offers.

PRO TIP: Using an online scheduling calendar to book appointments can shave WEEKS off back-and-forth e-mail messages that read something like, "I'm not free on Wed. Does Fri. work?" or "That doesn't work. How about the 16th at 4 p.m. ET?" . . . and on it goes.

But don't stop now! Here are a few more jewels you can use to develop your follow-up campaign. Remember that over 90 percent will NOT reply to your first message — so you must be persistent and constantly reach out with creative and personal follow-ups when you're going for an individual contact.

E-mail #2:

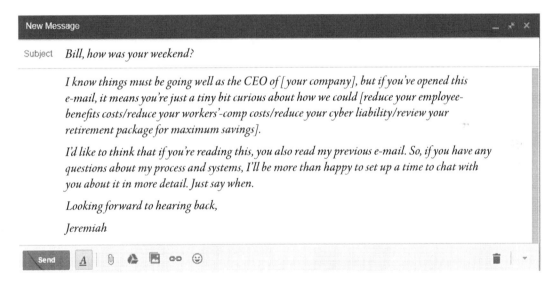

Then, keep going.

Here's E-mail #3:

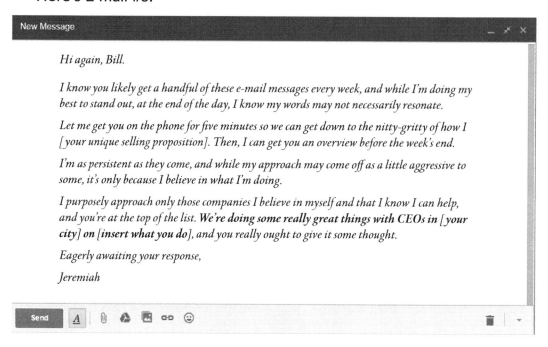

Hi again, Bill.

I know you likely get a handful of these e-mail messages every week, and while I'm doing my best to stand out, at the end of the day, I know my words may not necessarily resonate.

Let me get you on the phone for five minutes so we can get down to the nitty-gritty of how I [your unique selling proposition]. Then, I can get you an overview before the week's end.

I'm as persistent as they come, and while my approach may come off as a little aggressive to some, it's only because I believe in what I'm doing.

I purposely approach only those companies I believe in myself and that I know I can help, and you're at the top of the list. **We're doing some really great things with CEOs in [your city] on [insert what you do]**, and you really ought to give it some thought.

Eagerly awaiting your response,

Jeremiah

And then, of course, there's E-mail #4:

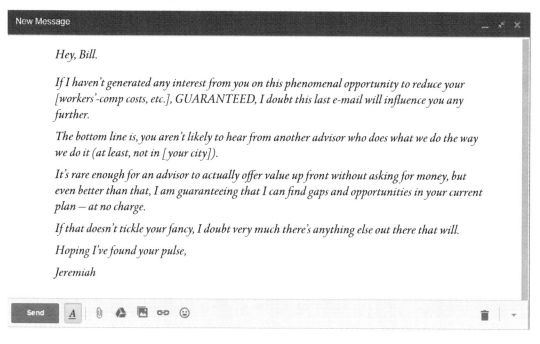

Hey, Bill.

If I haven't generated any interest from you on this phenomenal opportunity to reduce your [workers'-comp costs, etc.], GUARANTEED, I doubt this last e-mail will influence you any further.

The bottom line is, you aren't likely to hear from another advisor who does what we do the way we do it (at least, not in [your city]).

It's rare enough for an advisor to actually offer value up front without asking for money, but even better than that, I am guaranteeing that I can find gaps and opportunities in your current plan — at no charge.

If that doesn't tickle your fancy, I doubt very much there's anything else out there that will.

Hoping I've found your pulse,

Jeremiah

And if those e-mail messages don't do the trick, this last message garnered a 6 percent response rate — even from C-suite members (CEOs, CFOs, CIOs, etc.), who we were afraid wouldn't appreciate the humor.

One financial advisor tried it out while contacting attendees of his Social Security seminar. He got ten responses in fifteen minutes! And he booked three appointments with people who hadn't replied to any of his previous e-mail messages!

E-mail #5:

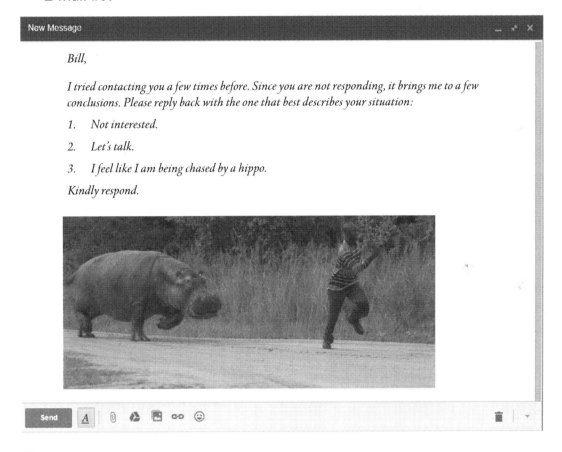

Bill,

I tried contacting you a few times before. Since you are not responding, it brings me to a few conclusions. Please reply back with the one that best describes your situation:

1. *Not interested.*
2. *Let's talk.*
3. *I feel like I am being chased by a hippo.*

Kindly respond.

Summary

In this chapter you got an insider's template perfectly designed to target power partnerships in difficult-to-reach positions. It can even be used to target the C-suite inside major corporations. This series of carefully crafted letters has resulted in eighty leads and eight appointments in a twenty-day window!

The key to reaching hard-to-reach people is sending a letter that stands out from the pack — and then following it up with more e-mail messages that do the same at every engagement.

The Takeaway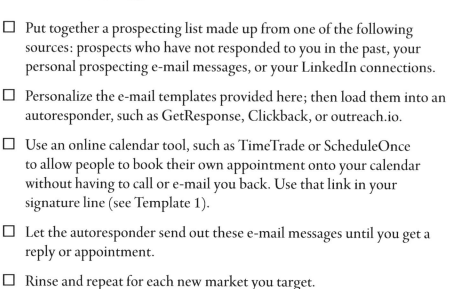

☐ Put together a prospecting list made up from one of the following sources: prospects who have not responded to you in the past, your personal prospecting e-mail messages, or your LinkedIn connections.

☐ Personalize the e-mail templates provided here; then load them into an autoresponder, such as GetResponse, Clickback, or outreach.io.

☐ Use an online calendar tool, such as TimeTrade or ScheduleOnce to allow people to book their own appointment onto your calendar without having to call or e-mail you back. Use that link in your signature line (see Template 1).

☐ Let the autoresponder send out these e-mail messages until you get a reply or appointment.

☐ Rinse and repeat for each new market you target.

CHAPTER 7

Smarter Marketing with Lifetime Customer Value Formula

"The result of long-term relationships is better and better quality, and lower and lower costs."
—W. Edwards Deming

Application: B2B, B2C
Difficulty: Easy
Time to implement: Thirty minutes
Cost to implement: Free

Having helped to build one of the largest insurance lead-generation companies in the country, I've heard practically every argument and excuse for why leads don't work. And they usually come from advisors and agents who don't understand the basic premise of Customer Lifetime Value (CLV).

In this chapter, I give you a primer in CLV and how to use it to make the SHIFT from penny-pinching advisor to savvy insurance and financial marketer.

How Much Does the Lead Cost?

If you've ever purchased leads, I bet your number-one metric was cost per lead. "What's the cost?" you ask the sales rep. What you may not realize, though, is that this is an <u>outdated metric that just isn't useful if you really want to play in the big leagues with the rest of us.</u>

If you're only thinking of cost per lead, you're limiting the way you grow your business. Also, more often than not, most lead opportunities look like failures. You'll never pursue them. You'll never take risks. And you'll stay small.

But there is a better way!

It's called "cost per acquisition." It's much more strategic to SHIFT your view away from CPL and toward CPA — the cost of acquiring a customer. Once you know that and you combine it with the Customer Lifetime Value (CLV), you'll really know your numbers. You'll be unstoppable.

I know one agent who had a breakthrough when he calculated his CLV. He took over his market in under six months, beating out his competitors, who were stuck on CPL Thinking.

<u>Lifetime Customer Value is the long-term revenue your agency gains from one new client.</u>

In other words, CLV is the key to predicting how much revenue a customer will bring you over the life of his business with you. To help you apply this to your own business, I'm going to show you the formula and how to use it.

Then, we'll review how one benefits agent calculated her CLV for the very first time.

BONUS: You can download a simple Excel sheet to use on www.TheShiftNation.org to help you along.

And then, I'll show you how to do it yourself.

The Formula

Average annual commission per deal X average time a customer stays with you - amount spent to acquire that customer = Lifetime Customer Value

Let's say your average annual premium for a typical sale is around $20,000.

Your average commission is 15 percent, or $3,000 per year for the average sale.

Then, let's assume this account buys from you once a year, and you keep the business for around five years.

Multiply the average annual commission by the number of years you'll hang onto the account. Set that number aside.

Now you need to calculate the cost of acquiring a new customer (CPA).

To keep it simple, let's just calculate the cost to generate the lead. It could be from radio, the Internet, television, or another media outlet.

For the purpose of this exercise, let's say you have to call on five leads that cost $100 each to get one new client.

That means you're spending an average of $500 on new-customer acquisition.

Subtract that number from the earlier number.

So, for a $20,000 account, you paid $500 and got paid $3,000.

If a customer brings in $3,000 a year in commission and you keep him for five years, that's a customer value of $15,000, minus your original cost of acquisition of $500 . . . *for a total lifetime customer value of $14,500.*

So, for a cost of $500, you were able to get a client who brought in $15,000.

Putting This Formula to Use in Your Marketing Strategy

The best part about this formula is that you can play around with the different factors.

If you want to see the customer's value if he only sticks around for two years, you can change that part of the formula, and you'll get a lifetime customer value of $5,500.

This highlights the importance of hanging onto that customer for as long as possible.

Knowing the CLV number shows you exactly how much it costs to acquire a customer and exactly how much he will earn you over the course of a year.

Once you know the value of your investment, you can market much more strategically.

You can create your own threshold.

A smart advisor who has made the SHIFT can say, "I'm going to make $7,000 over the course of this customer's time with me, so based on my other expenses, I'm comfortable spending $1,000 to acquire his business."

And if you double that investment, you can be confident that your earnings will respond accordingly.

In short, knowing your Lifetime Customer Value makes your budgeting decisions much more clear. Your goals will be grounded in reality.

Put another way, imagine there was a slot machine in your office and every time you put in a dime, a quarter came out, guaranteed! How many dimes would you put into that machine?

As many as you could, right?

That's the same kind of thinking that smart marketers adopt. They don't get hung up on cost per lead because that's limited thinking. They think in broader, more expansive terms.

A Sad—but True—Story

I once coached a very nice woman who wanted to "generate a TON of high-net-worth prospects immediately and cheaply" (her words, not mine).

When we sat down to take a look at the current postcard campaigns she was running, she was paying roughly $500 to run the campaign, and she was earning an average of $5,000 every month. Even when her monthly mailing wasn't successful, the law of averages remained intact and she still had that incredible ROI.

It was a fantastic return on investment: ten times ROI!

But that ten-to-one return on investment wasn't good enough for her, and she continued to search for the next "magic shiny object" that would bring her "faster and cheaper leads."

Shame on her. And shame on us if we don't SHIFT our thinking TODAY and begin to look at our marketing world in a more profitable light.

Summary

If you want to think more strategically and play a bigger game, you need to think in terms of the long-term value of a client. If you understand that, you can outmaneuver would-be competitors who get stuck on small-time metrics such as cost per lead.

If you can SHIFT to this type of reasoning as you move through this book, you'll open up doors of opportunity for yourself. Windfalls of profits are sure to follow.

The Takeaway

- ☐ Calculate your Lifetime Customer Value using the formula above.

- ☐ Play with the numbers: What if you held onto a client for a longer (or shorter) time? What if you spent more (or less) on marketing?

- ☐ Now calculate how much it would cost you to acquire a new client.

- ☐ Make all your future marketing decisions based on that metric and ruthlessly stick to it. *Make more powerful decisions using that metric.*

Book Bonus! Log in to the private Members area to download an Excel sheet that will help you calculate your CLV and make smarter marketing decisions. Go to www.Theshiftnation.org.

CHAPTER 8

Selling While You Sleep with Simple Online Systems and Tools

"Don't let what you cannot do interfere with what you can do."
—John R. Wooden

Application: B2C
Difficulty: Easy
Time to implement: Two-plus hours
Cost to implement: $10+

I love a family-run business that strives for the highest level of support.

So when I met one of the family members who's running Starmount Life and heard their story, I knew it was a story I wanted to include in this manual for you to learn two powerful lessons from:

1. Even in the digital age, a personal accountability to service trumps all.
2. Even long-established businesses can evolve and grow with the times if they keep the entrepreneurial mind-set that kept them there.

The Sternberg family has been in private, family-owned business over two hundred years. At first, they started in a retail business and owned twenty-four department stores in Louisiana and Florida.

One of the departments within the department stores was an insurance-agency carrier that had term life insurance.

Another was a credit card department that — get this — didn't charge interest!

So they had six hundred thousand very loyal credit card holders they would offer term life insurance to via statement stuffers. A client would get his credit card statement and then in there, would be statement stuffers offering them life insurance.

When the Sternberg family sold the stores in the early '90s, the purchaser of the department store wanted nothing to do with insurance due to its high level of regulation.

They asked Mr. Sternberg if he wanted to keep the insurance piece of the department stores, to which he responded, "Sure." And so, Starmount Life Insurance was born.

What I love about their model is that they continued the retail mind-set even in insurance: high touch, high service. In fact, when one does business with Starmount, it's surprisingly easy to get to senior management. (Is your firm structured that way?)

It's this high-touch mentality that gave birth to one of the key innovations in the last few years at Starmount, which we'll jump into next.

The Birth of the Starmount "Selling While You Sleep" Strategy

Once upon a time, Starmount Insurance Company had two sides to their business: employee benefits and individual benefits. The two sides never met.

As health-care reform began to change the market, Starmount built three different websites for their individual sector:

1. Dental and vision
2. AB&D
3. Juvenile-life-insurance plans

On the back end, they structured these sites similarly to what you'd see on Amazon. You visit the dental site (dentalforall.com), and see several dental-plan choices. From there, you can compare them, select one, and add it to your cart. Then, there's a simple three-step process to enroll in the plan.

And once you enter your payment information, as long as you are accepted, the policy is issued right then and there.

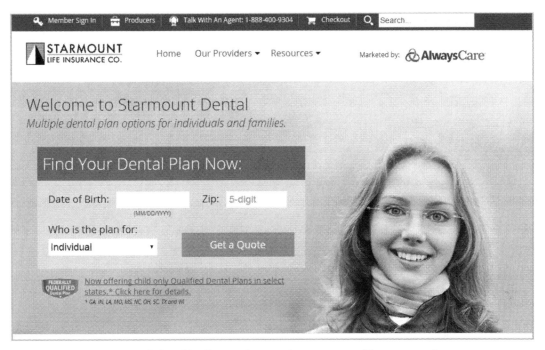

Starmount's dentalforall.com website can be set up as an affiliate page, such as www.dentalforall.com/yourid for easy, automated digital sales.

So how can something like this help brokers?

Well, Starmount issued custom links for their agents. They call this the "Selling While You Sleep" Strategy. The customer follows the link from the agent's website, and since the company can track the source, they issue commissions accordingly.

As health-care reform complicates the market and brokers focus more on major medical at the expense of supplemental benefits, Starmount's system helps agents add these offerings to their product mix with no additional effort.

Over a thousand brokers are now using these links and selling hundreds of policies a week. In 2015, Starmount was on track to close 230 percent more business than they did in 2014.

Starmount is a smaller carrier, which would seem to put them at a disadvantage. But it's their size that allows them to do innovative things like this — to stay nimble and respond quickly to their agents' changing needs.

They can also pay attention to details such as creating a responsive website specifically for their youth life product. That site is easy to navigate and use from a PC, smartphone, or other mobile device.

A Simple Cross-sell with No Additional Effort

One firm came to Starmount from a different carrier, an individual dental provider that was exiting the market.

Within three minutes, their custom site was up and running. Within three months, they had sold thirteen hundred policies through the site.

The best part is that tools like this can be used by agencies both big and small. It can be used by individual agents. Even if you're selling face-to-face, it can be added as a supplement to your main way of doing business.

As an upselling or cross-selling mechanism, it can't be beat.

The Takeaway 👍

☐ Make a list of the lines of business you can add as a complement to your primary products.

☐ Look for ways to streamline selling those ancillary lines. Can you use a system like Starmount's, where sign-up is simplified and can be accomplished entirely online? If not, look for other carriers that can offer similar complementary offerings.

☐ Use these additional lines as an upsell or cross-sell for primary products. For instance, a new life customer might be interested in a youth-life product for his child.

CHAPTER 9

The Sneaky, Forty-Seven-Dollar, White-Hat Google-Ranking-Solution System

"If you build it, they will come."
—Field of Dreams

Application: B2B, B2C
Difficulty: Easy
Time to implement: Thirty minutes
Cost to implement: $47 a month

Google processes more than forty thousand search queries every second.

That's more than 3.5 billion searches per day—or 1.2 trillion searches per year. (Internet Live Stats, 2014)

Each month, Google handles:

- 246,000 searches for "life insurance": 8,200 a day, 341 an hour, or five every minute

- 27,000 searches for "retirement planning": 900 a day, 37 an hour, one every two minutes

- 47,300 searches for "home insurance quote": 1,576 a day, 65 an hour, one every minute

- 430,000 searches for "auto insurance quote": 14,333 a day, 597 an hour, ten every minute

- 27,100 searches for "health insurance quote": 900 a day, 37 per hour, one every two minutes

Data as of October 2015, per Google Keyword Research Tool.

That's a surprising number of financial searches every minute.

In the US alone, every three-and-a-half seconds someone is searching for some variety of insurance or financial services! (Tweet that!)

And that's just on Google; it doesn't even include searches conducted on Bing or Yahoo! Consider the following statistics:

- Nearly two in three mass affluent consumers take action after using social media to discover and consider financial products and services. (The DigitalFA)

- Two out of three millionaires would like to use electronic media with their advisors. (The DigitalFA)

- Almost every mass affluent consumer uses social media (90 percent). And nearly half of them — 44 percent — engage with financial institutions on social media. (LinkedIn)

- 89 percent of consumers search for products using search engines. (PR Newswire)

- 72 percent of consumers trust online reviews as much as personal recommendations from people they know. (Search Engine Journal)

- Inbound marketing costs 62 percent less per lead than traditional outbound marketing. (Groove Digital Marketing)

- 28 percent of Internet usage is conducted on a mobile phone.

This handy Google infographic shows the times of year when people search most in the financial category. Not surprisingly, January is prime time for searches on mortgages, retirement, and savings.

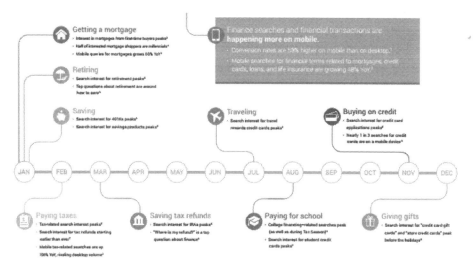

Source: http://storage.googleapis.com/think/docs/finance-trends-throughout-the-year.pdf

So, they're looking.

But, How do you get SEEN by all these shopping consumers?

There are ten thousand baby boomers retiring every day.

That's sixty million-plus boomers trying to figure out how best to leverage their financial investments over the next fifteen to twenty years. The majority of them will look for guidance on the Internet — many preferring to do business with a LOCAL agent.

Yet many agents I speak with still do not have a website, and the ones who do are not seeing much traffic.

What's the point of having a website if it doesn't get traffic that generates new business?

Although this entire chapter could be dedicated to the *right* way to do search engine optimization, Google algorithm updates would quickly make it obsolete.

There's a simple solution to local searches.

Here's a simple solution if you want *local* searches to come to you: AdvisorRank.

Full disclosure: AdvisorRank is a business I have financial stake in. So if you use their service, I may receive some form of compensation.

This simple and extremely affordable monthly service drives local traffic, consisting of people searching for help in their area, to local agents' websites.

Agents receive prime exposure on page one of the top thirty search-engine websites driving traffic to the agents' website.

Now that traffic is flowing, you have to ask: Is your website primed to generate leads?

A "Better Than a Website" Alternative

You may know that a website with no call to action beyond a "Contact Us" page serves no purpose.

The whole reason for traffic is to generate new business. And the only way to generate that business is to speak with the interested party.

If your website doesn't include your phone number or lead forms in multiple areas, you really have no avenue for communication.

It's crucial to lure the visitor to call you to receive a free marketing piece, or fill out a form and download a retirement guide. There's your door-opener to the sale.

Using AdvisorRank, you can set up a simple, three-page website that is ranked locally *and* converts traffic. It even includes a brief but high-end educational video.

If you were to tackle your website from scratch, it would take weeks. Then you'd need to worry about getting yourself ranked highly on the thirty-plus local search engines that feed into Google searches (each requiring its own unique username and password).

AdvisorRank's solution does it all, for just $47 a month.

Here's a sample:

Sample template of a local lead-generation website set up within
twenty-four hours for just $47.

How much premium has been sold using this technique? On average, an agent will receive 520 annual unique website visits.

Of those, some will become leads worth between $25 and $60 each.

In total, this strategy has generated more than $1 in AUM (Assets Under Management) from just a handful of advisors on the platform.

One agency's website was floundering in cyberspace. This tool helped them grow their presence on all local search engines, as well as on Google Local, Maps, and Plus. As a result, their lead conversion rate has gone up significantly.

The thirty local search engines that Google relies on most to source local businesses.

Another agent's website attracted hundreds of local prospects searching for retirement and investment guidance just one year after deploying this service. His website is now a true lead generator, bringing in qualified leads that lead to in-person meetings with interested clients — boosting his sales today and ensuring future revenue, as well.

The Takeaway 👆

- ☐ Consider your web presence: not just the existence of your website, but its optimization and its ranking in search.

- ☐ Check out a tool, such as AdvisorRank, that can help you build a rich, effective website. You can learn more about it at www.Theshiftnation.org.

- ☐ Continually monitor your website traffic and analytics to ensure ongoing optimization.

CHAPTER 10

The Two-Dollar Water Bottle Trick to Get Life-Insurance Leads

"Make a customer, not a sale."
—Katherine Barchetti

Application: B2C
Difficulty: Easy
Time to implement: One hour
Cost to implement: $12

Here's a simple strategy anyone can use to build leads within a morning. You may have to step a bit out of your comfort zone for it, but there is really no cheaper way I've ever heard of to generate life-insurance leads.

It comes from a friend and very enterprising life-insurance agent, Mark Rosenthal. Mark adapted an old church recruitment strategy to garner more appointments.

Here's how he tells it:

> *I went to Sam's Club and bought some small water bottles. I printed my basic info onto size 5160 Avery labels and stuck them to the water bottles.*
>
> *Then, I went to the local walking track here in Griffin, by the airport. I chose the track because most of the people there are trying to lose weight or stay healthy, and many are in great shape.*
>
> *Then, I started doing something I learned from my church recruitment days: I just walked up to people and offered them a cold bottle of water. Most accepted.*
>
> *I didn't try to stop them in their tracks or take up too much of their time. I just told them that, because they were out there exercising, they might be able to get*

a discount on life insurance. Then I asked if I could show them the type of rate I could offer them.

One lady had just lost over forty pounds. She went from a Table 2 to Preferred. If someone had given her a quote before she'd lost the weight, she would have been quoted a Table 2 instead of her new class.

One lady was super healthy and it was hard to keep up with her pace. After talking to her for a minute, I knew she would be Super Preferred.

I was able to get three appointments out of just two hours of walking and around six dollars' worth of water.

I've always said that it's all about seeing the people. You have to get out, be seen, and interact with people. My goal was to do some walking, spend a little bit of money, and see if I could set some appointments.

How to SHIFT This Strategy Online to Reach Thousands More

This tactic works wonders online too.

Buy Facebook ads and target people who "like" fitness-related pages, for example, Beachbody, CrossFit, Jenny Craig, and Weight Watchers.

If I were doing this, I'd show "before and after" pictures — a massive eye-grabber — accompanied by a headline such as:

Have you lost more than twenty pounds on Beachbody? Then, you're probably paying too much for life insurance!

Watch this free informational video now, and learn one weird trick to save more money.

When people clicked on the ad, it would send them to a simple page featuring a blog about how to save money after weight loss and a form to fill out for more information.

Now, Use This Approach on Even More Prospects—Offline

Here's another option:

Have a virtual assistant contact all the personal trainers in your town.

Write a template e-mail, something like this:

I noticed you're a personal trainer in the area, and thought I'd reach out about a potential business alliance.

I specialize in helping people who have lost more than twenty pounds to get better discounts on their life and health insurance.

Most people don't know this, but when insurance companies set a price for a person's plan, they base it on his or her body mass index (BMI).

So, when people start taking care of themselves and losing weight, they should always get an updated quote — and usually, their premium will go down.

I've seen this save people hundreds of dollars a year. Multiply that times several years, and it's thousands in savings.

I'd like to refer some of my clients to you to get in better shape. In turn, I hope you can do the same for me with your clients who lose weight.

I'd be happy to pay you a fee for every new client you find me.

Let me know if this might be of interest to you.

Regards,
Susan

You can approach gyms and fitness clubs with the same offer. Ask them if you can make a presentation one day or set up a table. Ask them to post flyers in the locker rooms or on the bulletin board. The possibilities are endless.

Remember, what works offline can work online too — and vice versa.

The Takeaway

- ☐ Get a small case of water and head over to a track where your community likes to work out. Then use Mark's strategy.

- ☐ Place ads on social networks that target fans of fitness programs. Invite them to get an updated quote based on their new body mass index (BMI).

- ☐ Contact local personal trainers, gyms, and fitness clubs and offer a partnership.

- ☐ Anytime you encounter a strategy that works well online, try a version of it offline. The same goes for an online strategy; SHIFT it offline and see what happens.

Bonus: You can access more ideas from Mark from the bonus section of the book. Log on to www.Theshiftnation.org to download them.

CHAPTER 11

Treat Your Clients to a Movie Night

*"Wanting something is not enough. You must hunger for it.
Your motivation must be absolutely compelling in order
to overcome the obstacles that will invariably come your way."*
—Les Brown

Application: B2B, B2C
Difficulty: Easy
Time to implement: One hour
Cost to implement: $30+

Sometimes you don't need any technology to generate leads. All you need to do is tap into people's universal desire to be entertained.

Tom Hegna has transformed his practice by branding himself with books, DVDs, and programs based on his Don't Worry, Retire Happy! brand. Recently, he sent me a note showing me what one of his clients is doing with his DVDs:

> *Jamie Norvell in Louisville, KY, put together a movie night in a bucket for clients, complete with popcorn, drinks, candy, and a copy of my DVD.*
>
> *Let ME show your friends why they need life insurance, annuities, and long-term care insurance.*

Can you do something similar for *your* clients?

Even if you don't have your own branded DVDs, you could create a short video. And if you don't want to mail it out in a bucket, you could send the video out with a digital gift certificate to Target or Amazon for a box of popcorn.

CHAPTER 12

How to Crowdsource Your Advantage Using Associations

"Outstanding people have one thing in common:
an absolute sense of mission."
—Zig Ziglar

Application: B2B, B2C
Difficulty: Easy
Time to implement: One hour
Cost to implement: $300+ a year

One of the biggest benefits of joining an association is having somebody on your side.

The insurance industry is ever-changing and, in ways, much more difficult than it used to be.

New legislation or regulations, industry trends, and more — it's important to stay abreast of everything affecting your business, but it's almost impossible to keep track on your own.

By joining an association, you can leverage the collective brain power, resources, research, and lobbying efforts of a small group of people for just a few hundred or thousand dollars per year.

Plus, many associations serve as an advocate for the agent, meeting with lawmakers and regulators and lobbying for the outcome that best serves advisors *and* clients.

I've been a member of several associations and found in each one great people who truly care about advancing the cause of insurance and financial services.

A Community of Like-minded Professionals

National Association of Health Underwriters (NAHU) is one of these associations. Martin Carr, editor of its official publication, *HIU* magazine, says he's drawn to the sense of camaraderie.

"Sure, it can be strange at first to think about sharing ideas in a room with the competition," says Martin. But he goes on to say that a funny thing happens once you become involved with a local chapter or national event. "All that stuff about the competition just sort of goes away, and everybody sees the greater good."

Some of the benefits of joining NAHU, in particular, include:

- A partnership with CMS to facilitate certification training for the Health Insurance Marketplace (it's the only agent-and-broker organization with such a program)
- Federal and state lobbying power
- Access to designations such as RHU and REBC
- Extensive resources in the Online Learning Institute
- Annual Capitol Conference in D.C.

Those are some of NAHU's specific benefits, but it's also just great being in a room full of people who have the same passions and ideals that you have," says Martin. "It's just [great] to be with your peers, and then to talk to somebody and know that they get exactly what you're talking about."

All the News That's Fit to Print

Associations also are a great source of information from tons of sources.

NAHU, in particular, gives members access to *HIU* magazine (which happens to include occasional articles by yours truly), along with a daily industry news blast, legislative newsletters, regulation updates, and more.

In the end, you can't really beat the power of an association such as NAHU.

"You talk to those people, I guarantee you almost every single one of them will say, 'This changed the way that I see my industry and what I do,'" Martin says.

The Takeaway 👍

☐ If you're a health insurance agent, consider visiting NAHU to learn more about membership (www.NAHU.org).

☐ Not a health insurance agent? There's still an organization for you. Just Google "insurance association" or "financial advisor association" to find one that serves your needs.

☐ Get involved in a local or regional chapter.

☐ Take advantage of all of the resources these associations have to offer. The price of membership is often a bargain!

Book Bonus: I've compiled a list of the top thirty-plus associations for insurance and financial advisors today. Download it now to find the one that's right for you: www.Theshiftnation.org.

CHAPTER 13

Tapping Into Leadership, Strength and Yes, SEO - for Non-Captive Agencies

Coming together is a beginning; keeping together is progress; working together is success.
—Henry Ford

The Independent Insurance Agents & Brokers of America (Big "I") is a national alliance of more than a quarter million business owners and their employees who offer all types of insurance and financial services products.

Per their website:

"Unlike company-employed agents, Big "I" independent insurance agents and insurance brokers represent more than one insurance company, so they can offer clients a wider choice of auto, home, business, life, health coverages as well as retirement and employee-benefit products."

They're a strong fit for Non-Captives.

A Smithsonian of Resources for Independent Agents

I have to hand it to the Big I. They have done an incredible job of understanding you and delivering in depth content to help agents (particularly P&C agents) get market advantages.

From Agency Management Best Practices to Technology to being a voice for young agents, they have got you covered.

Showing Love To The Up And Comers (Yes, there ARE Young agents Succeeding!)

One of the areas that is often neglected in our industry is the nurturing of young talent and encouragement of attracting young talent into this industry. With over 60% of our industry retiring in the next seven years, this is an urgent issue.

The Big I has tackled this head on.

The Big "I" National Young Agents Committee (YAC) encourages Young Agents – those under 40 years of age or with less than 5 years experience in the industry – to become aware of and get involved in the activities and programs of the Independent Insurance Agents & Brokers of America (the Big "I").

They hold engaging events all over the country and an annual leadership conference for idea sharing and supporting this fast growing demographic this industry sorely needs.

Investing the in the future of Youth

In addition, they have created the InVEST program that I had the pleasure of being a part of.

InVEST, a school-to-work insurance program, teams with high school and college educators to provide a useful insurance curriculum for students. In addition to learning the principals of insurance, with the help of InVEST liaisons (insurance professionals), students could have the opportunity for job shadow days, internships or even careers after graduating from InVEST.

Guest speakers during an InVEST class provide firsthand knowledge of what it's like to work in the insurance field, and students have a new appreciation for the industry after a hearing a professional speak. And, before you've even entered the room they already are excited to have someone other than their teacher speaking to them! Sorry Mrs. Crabapple.

Getting the Best from the Best - The Best Practice Study

Some time back through my role as Vice President of Marketing with Applied Systems, I had the privilege of working with the Big I through the "Best Practices" study.

The Best Practices Study was initiated by the Big "I" in 1993 as the foundation for efforts to improve agency performance and create higher valued agencies. The survey and study of leading independent insurance agencies documents the business practices of these "best" agencies and urges others to adopt similar practices. This way you get direct access to strategies that are working right now.

Every three years, the Big "I" collaborates with Reagan Consulting to select "Best Practices" firms throughout the nation for outstanding management and financial achievement in six revenue categories (less than $1,250,000; $1,250,000 to $2,500,000; $2,500,000 to $5,000,000; $5,000,000 to $10,000,000; $10,000,000 to $25,000,000; and more than $25,000,000). I like this approach as it balances success by production level.

Agencies are nominated by either a Big "I"-affiliated state association or an insurance company and qualified based on operational excellence, so the nomination process is fair.

How Top Agents spend their time - How do you stack up?

Studies like the "Best Practices" create help us all raise our game. For example, in their 2015 study, they discovered how successful producers spend their time:

8.3% in Professional Development

18.2% in Agency Management

28.6% in Soliciting New Business (my favorite area of activity ;-)

44.9% in Servicing Existing Accounts

How do your producers stack up?

Black, Latino, Asian and every beautiful color in between

Having spent the majority of my life living among and helping people who were not born here through my volunteer work, I'm a big fan of diversity. I grew in Montreal, one of the most ethnically diverse cities in the world. A city where you never know if the person in front of you is going to speak Haitian Creole, Urdu, Hmong, Arabic, French, Thai, Chinese or Jamaican Patois. It's wonderful.

In an industry that has been self-admittedly 'mainly white', the Big I has taken a stand here to help build bridges to and awareness around diversity.

The Big "I" Diversity Task Force is a cooperative industry group comprised of Big "I" members representing Latin-American, African-American and Asian-American agents in addition, leading insurance company executives from Chubb, CNA, Encompass, Erie, Hartford, Liberty Mutual Insurance, MetLife Auto & Home, Nationwide, Safeco, Selective Insurance Company of America and Travelers.

The Diversity Task Force collaborates with other multicultural industry groups, state associations and other Big "I" committees to create an awareness of the opportunities and benefits available by embracing diversity and encouraging change necessary for the independent agency system to survive and flourish.

Mr. Agent Goes To Washington

Per the Big I, as the federal government exercises more regulatory power over financial services, the future of the insurance market is becoming dependent on agents' ability to engage in the federal political process. InsurPac is the federal political action committee (PAC) for independent agents and it works hand in hand with the association's advocacy efforts. As a multi million dollar PAC, it is among the top one tenth of one percent of all federal PACs in terms of size and effectiveness.

InsurPac uses its size to develop Big "I" relationships with members of the U.S. House, Senate and candidates for federal office.

The Lead Generating Power of TrustedChoice.com

Some time ago the Big I spawned TrustedChoice.com, which is not a subsidiary of the association but an independently owned and operated web marketing platform 100% dedicated to helping insurance shoppers find the right independent insurance agent for them and their family or business.

It's one of the largest independent P&C marketing platform on the web, seeing approximately 5 million P&C insurance shoppers per year (personal, commercial, life and health).

Subscribers get a complete agency profile which is tuned to their sales appetite so they are put in front of the customers they want most, and tuned to their appointed carriers.

This means that if a shoppers that prefers Safeco over Travelers, they'll find a Safeco agent. So your chances of converting that lead are much higher.

When you sign up to TrustedChoice.com for $59 a month, you get an SEO optimized page complete with video, Google map integration, full contact details and more.

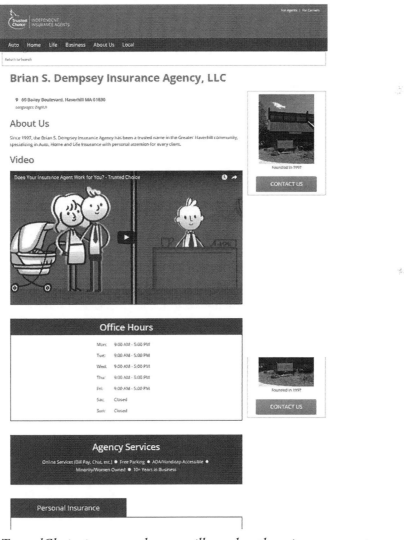

What a TrustedChoice insurance shopper will see when they view your agent page on TrustedChoice.com

This 'online hub' of traffic helps not only the agency website appear higher in search results but also each agency profile on TrustedChoice.com also appears as a search results link, often on page one of google. It's a strong value that wins agents new traffic, leads and clients.

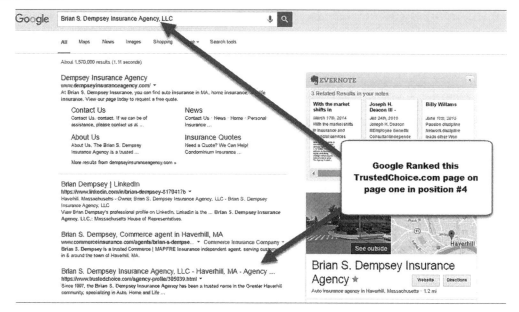

Google ranked this agent's website on page in position #4
for the name of this agency

They've also included a feature that creates a link back from TrustedChoice.com to the agency website. A link back from an authoritative website like this improves the agent's site search engine value, which is great for SEO. Any independent agent can start driving more traffic and inbound business to their agency by taking 30 minutes to create an Advantage agency profile on TrustedChoice.com for as little as $59 per month.

When we tested this theory out, not only did the agency NAME rank on page 1, but also a very specific keyword search for a "Haverhill Mass Insurance Agency". Their agency site ranked even HIGHER, dominating at Position #2. Here's where you can see the power of backlinks working their magic.

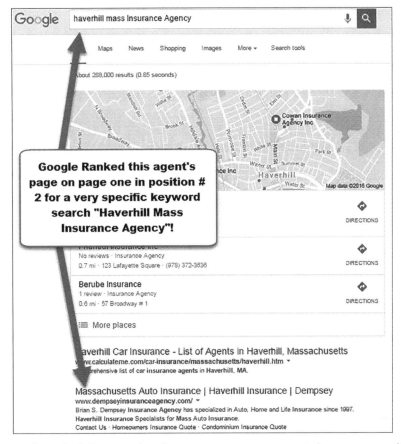

Google ranked this agent's website on page in position #2 for a very specific search string "Haverhill Mass Insurance Agency" which is harder to rank for.

In many cases, agents can get their subscription to TrustedChoice.com paid for in part or in whole by their insurance carriers. 62 P&C insurance companies participate on TrustedChoice.com including most of the big names like Safeco, Liberty Mutual, Travelers, Hartford, CNA, Metlife, Hanover, etc. In addition, many regional and one or two state carriers participate as well.

According to Chip Bacciocco, President of Trusted Choice (a program of the Independent Insurance Agents and Brokers of America, Inc. There are even further advantages of being part of an association of like-minded agents and advisors.

For example, becoming a member of TrustedChoice.com gives incredible brand recognition and a competitive advantage over other agents - highlighting the fact you are independent and not tied to certain carriers. Consumers like this "you're working for me "positioning.

In addition, being a member increases visibility online by being listed in their national directory of agents on TrustedChoice.com which gets thousands of visitors a week looking for agents. This generates traffic and more importantly - leads - for member agents.

Try this:

☐ Check out www.independentagent.com and view their resources to see if their membership is a good fit for your non-captive model

☐ Visit www.trustedchoice.com/for-agents to sign up for their online listing membership

☐ Attend a local meeting of the Big "I" and get involved with your industry. A complete listing can be found here http://www.independentagent.com/Events/Pages/Calendars/default.aspx (sorry for the Cryptic link!)

CHAPTER 14

Leads Today: Trends, Strategies, and Tips for Success

"Take risks. Ask the dumb questions.
Fail if you have to, and then get up and do it again."
—Jaqueline Novogratz, entrepreneur

Before we get into it, just a note that you're doing GREAT. I've given you a lot of information so far, and you're still trucking right along. I'm proud of what you've put into practice right now, and you're well on your way to making your own personal *SHIFT*.

As we get into more advanced techniques, it's good to come up for a air for a moment to appreciate what's happening right now in the world of financial lead generation.

Internet lead generation is a great way to find qualified customers. It's a common strategy in the insurance world.

Over the past fifteen years, Internet leads have evolved as consumer habits change.

It's been estimated that more than 85 percent of insurance buyers start their research and shopping online. So, love them or hate them, insurance leads are here to stay.

Internet leads are changing in a lot of different ways, according to Mark Wheeler. Mark is an authority on insurance lead generation and the former vice president of marketing for NetQuote, one of the largest generators of insurance leads in the country.

Evolving Rules of Engagement

Consumers are more self-directed and have access to more information than ever before.

Technology allows them to research, select, and purchase products and services however they'd like.

But the consumer market is also quite segmented. Millennials and baby boomers have totally different buying behavior. It's important to be able to reach your leads in ways that resonate with them.

Expanded Lead Generation

Lead providers capture information in lots of ways. Ad clicks, form fills, cold calling, e-mail — all of these have traditionally filled the funnel.

Today, traditional methods are still being used but in brand-new ways.

Super click, click-to-call, warm lead transfers, social media, mobile, and video have begun to complement older methods such as direct mail, referrals, and affinity relationships.

Mobile

Mobile is arguably the most important lead-generation trend. It's simple: if you're not thinking of mobile, you will be left behind.

For the first time in history, mobile searches have outpaced desktop searches. So your website simply has to be optimized for mobile.

This means employing a simple, clean layout and responsive design. Consider using a template that is already optimized for mobile and can easily be updated on the go. You can find thousands that are ready to deploy for under $50 on themeforest.com.

Deciding on Your Ideal Lead-Generation Strategy

To generate or to buy? That is the question.

The decision of whether to outsource lead generation or create them yourself depends on a lot of factors:

- Your level of commitment
- Your resources
- How much you can afford to invest and risk
- Your long-term strategy

We discuss some lead-generation tactics later in the book. The bottom line is this: if you really want to become an expert and control the process, then do it yourself.

But if you'd rather focus on other areas of your business, consider outsourcing by buying leads.

Basic Lead-Generation Tactics

If you're new to lead generation, a third-party lead aggregator can give you quick access to leads with little effort.

These vendors provide immediate access to qualified leads based on your criteria — and they provide support to help you manage those leads, as well.

Whatever method you're using, you need to monitor its effectiveness. Keep track of how many leads you're generating and when. Determine the best days and times to deliver the leads for timely follow-up. And remember, the early agent gets the prospect.

Google Analytics is a free tool that can track your website activity. This is especially important when analyzing how leads from different sources are performing, and, in turn, when developing strategic marketing.

There are some other things to keep in mind:

- **Don't hide.** You have to make it easy for people to find you. Search engine optimization (SEO) is important. Google also offers more than twenty products that can help you build a back-end infrastructure for lead generation.
- **Optimize your site for local search.** Seventy-eight percent of all website visits come from an online search. A strong web presence is essential — and it's not enough just to have a website. Drive traffic with SEO and optimize your site with geography-specific keywords. Include these keywords where it matters most: in the page title, URL, header tags (H1, H2, etc.), body content, and on-page links. If you're not an expert, consider a service that can audit your site and provide guidance.
- **Optimize your site for conversion.** Once visitors hit your site, you want them to stay there and take action. Offer useful information that nurtures a relationship. Also include forms to contact you, and a call to action. (Later in this section, we discuss a quick landing-page tweak that can up your conversions.)

Follow-up: A Blueprint for Success

Regardless of how you're generating leads, proper follow-up is essential.

Contact leads as soon as you receive them. MIT studies have demonstrated that after one hour, your odds of catching that prospect decrease by more than ten times. Ideally, you're making three calls within the first two hours of lead generation.

The first call should be within a minute. Ideally, the agent makes this call, but if that's impossible, have a qualified admin screen the prospect. That person should then schedule a call or send an auto e-mail to confirm that you received the inquiry and will contact the interested party directly.

The second call should come within thirty minutes to an hour, and the third, between one and two hours after that. Make a fourth call on day five, a fifth on day fourteen, and a sixth on day fifteen.

Later, we'll get into more nitty-gritty details of exactly HOW to accomplish all of this. For now, I want to invite you to open your mind to the possibilities of how you can approach your ideal lead-generation strategy.

The Takeaway 👍

☐ Decide whether you want to generate your own leads or buy them/outsource the task.

☐ Set up a defined follow-up process that includes phone calls and e-mail messages.

☐ Test the process for effectiveness.

CHAPTER 15

The SHIFT of Online Lead-Generation Companies

"The majority of men meet with failure because of their lack of persistence in creating new plans to take the place of those which fail."
–Napoleon Hill

Application: B2B, B2C
Difficulty: Easy
Time to implement: One hour
Cost to implement: Varies based on volume

In the beginning, there was online lead generation.

This particular beginning occurred in the mid-2000s — a time when, according to Bill Daniel, CEO of All Web Leads, most agents were just beginning to discover the power of the Internet.

Their somewhat late adoption came at the same time that consumers were going online more and more frequently to research finances and insurance.

For agents developing an online presence at this time, there was suddenly a flood of prospects.

The only problem was, they all looked alike. The agent had no choice but to work them all equally — even those who would never go anywhere.

Coupled with low accountability, this lack of differentiation led to a lot of bad practices in the lead-generation industry, and an environment where agents just spent their money and hoped for the best.

"In the ten years since," says Bill, "we've come a long way. There's more accountability and oversight on the part of the buyers — the agents and the carriers."

Don't Call Them a Lead Generator

Bill represents a SHIFT himself. He refers to his company as a "customer-acquisition marketing business," not a "lead generator."

His number-one goal is to help agents acquire customers. This is a big change from the old way of thinking, he says, which was just stuffing leads into the top of the sales funnel.

"It doesn't do us any good to fill the funnel with no-intent or low-intent consumers," he explains. "Our customers, the agents and carriers, would spend too much time and energy following up for nothing."

Instead, Bill's company focuses on drawing consumers further down into the sales funnel.

One example is his call center.

There, leads are qualified and ranked in terms of intent. Staff members determine how well the leads meet an agent's ideal buyer profile. Then they transfer qualified customers to the agent, who gets to quote and, often, sell that customer on the spot.

Quadruple Your Close Rate

So how does this work out for Bill's clients?

One large P&C carrier Bill works with has shared some metrics.

Basically, Bill's company has three different products: data (leads), live call center (calls), and clicks.

This carrier uses his call product. For metrics, they're most interested in quote rate and close rate.

With calls, this carrier gets a 22 percent higher quote rate.

And the close rate?

Four times higher.

Why a Call Center Beats an Agent

Here's Bill's secret.

His call center takes leads they've generated through their website and calls those leads. This is the exact same thing an agent does when he purchases a lead. But when the call center does it, the contact rate is two times higher.

There are two reasons why:

1. Many agents don't call every single lead they get.
2. Many agents don't follow up as diligently as they should.

The call center, on the other hand, does both of those things very well.

Uncovering Buyer Intent

So how do you know which leads have a high buyer intent?

One big indicator, says Bill, is the keywords used when searching. For instance, a visitor who landed on their site from typing "affordable auto insurance" or "Allstate" has made it clear what he is looking for. His buying intent is high.

Another is the media source. By examining specific data, Bill knows where the lead is in the buying cycle based on where it came from.

Leads are handled based on whether they come from search, display, e-mail, or social media advertising. Differing-intent customers are qualified in different ways, and each lead is sent down a specific path optimized for conversion performance.

Bill also gets performance data directly from customers, creating a closed-loop feedback system.

"Our customers tell us which leads they quoted and which they sold, and because we're dealing with them on such a massive scale, we can take that data and, over time, build predictive models."

These models allow Bill to predict, in real-time, the intent of a consumer coming from a certain media source or ad campaign. His firm has a model for each advertising source, campaign, and customer category.

And that's what sets them apart from a mere lead generator.

How One Agent Turned Lackluster Leads into a Winning Strategy

Jeff Caufield is one agent who demonstrates the power of working leads effectively.

At first, he was tempted to give up on Internet leads. They weren't working and they cost too much. Then, he realized it was a numbers game and approached it anew.

"We analyzed the numbers, and then looked at how many items we really wanted to sell," Jeff says. "And then I figured out how many leads we'd have to buy in order to get that."

They started off with a goal of one hundred items (policies, etc.) sold. Now, three years later, their goal is over a thousand.

Today, Jeff is the number-one agent in New York and his is among the top ten Allstate agencies for new sales. He attributes 90 percent of his growth to a solid lead strategy.

"Leads are a very important part of your business," Jeff says. "You have to manage them, because they're just like your best employee. They're only as good as the effort you put into them."

Each day, Jeff reviews his quote/lead ratio and conversion ratio. He says most agents only look at conversions. And then they think the leads aren't working because they don't really understand the metrics they're looking at.

He also advocates choosing a lead manager with whom you can partner.

"You have to work together," Jeff says, "because if it's not profitable, it doesn't work for either of you."

How to Find High-Value Leads

If you're looking for a lead generator — or a "customer-acquisition marketer" — what might you ask to make sure you're getting the highest-intent lead with the most value?

1. **Look for calls, not transfers.** Start with the product with the highest close and quote rates, Bill says. Calls will cost more but have a much higher ROI.
2. **Ask about the vendor's feedback systems.** A vendor that creates, calls, and transfers the consumer to you tends to deliver much higher rates of success than vendors dialing leads generated elsewhere.

The Takeaway

☐ When looking for lead companies, consider whether you're buying calls or transfers, and the ROI on each.

☐ Look at where the leads are being generated. Is the company generating them? Or are they somebody else's lead? Do they have a closed-feedback system?

☐ Check allwebleads.com to see if they have lead options you can start testing.

CHAPTER 16

Boosting Closing Ratios by 30 Percent to 50 Percent Using Short-Term Medical Engines

"In order to be irreplaceable, one must always be different."
—Coco Chanel

Application: B2C
Difficulty: Moderate
Time to implement: One-week learning curve
Cost to implement: Free

The Affordable Care Act (ACA) marketplace would appear to be a formidable competitor for independent online and call-center models.

But when consumers see a number of online options for health insurance with no apparent differences among them, it can be tough to encourage them to choose yours.

What's more, some brokers turn around over 30 percent of inbound calls because they don't fit into the traditional ACA model. This is a huge revenue loss.

But there's a simple solution to not only recapture that lost revenue, but also boost closing ratios over 30 percent with this approach.

Enter the SHIFT to Short-term Medical

Scott Lingle offers a great example of a unique value proposition for models that are similar to ACA. Health Insurance Innovations (HII) provides short-term medical plans in forty-six states on an electronic platform with a call center.

They're big on technology, and among their innovations is a calculator that helps agents show prospects and clients their best options for coverage when comparing ACA plans to short-term medical.

"See, no matter how revolutionary, healthcare.gov can be very confusing. Consumers whose heads are spinning would do well to sit down with an agent who can provide a side-by-side comparison," says Scott.

Using Online Engines to Boost Sales

With HII's calculator, agents can calculate any subsidies the consumer qualifies for and the cost of an ACA plan for him. And with the product portfolio, they can offer affordable short-term medical alternatives in the event that the ACA option is just too expensive.

While the ACA does cover a large number of those previously uninsured — namely, the poor and sick — it has created another large pool of uninsured Americans. As Scott points out, this pool tends to be made up of younger single consumers with higher incomes. Since they may not qualify for a subsidy, the ACA plan may seem too costly to them, given that they are young and feel invincible.

While short-term medical plans may not cover items such as maternity or preventive care, or accept those with preexisting conditions, for the right people, this isn't necessarily a deal-breaker. And even when you factor in the ACA penalty (short-term medical doesn't meet its requirements for alternative health coverage), the premium savings often more than make up for it.

Scott encourages customers to align their short-term medical plan start and stop dates with open-enrollment periods.

Because short-term medical isn't guaranteed renewable, anybody who develops a condition over its twelve-month term may not be able to renew. In that case, since they've set their expiration date to coincide with open enrollment, they can seek other plans or sign up for ACA.

Anecdotally, Scott says an average closing ratio when using this type of approach can reach anywhere from 30 to 50 percent.

It's all because you're able to serve a much broader audience than before.

Scott has found that during open enrollment, anywhere from 30 to 40 percent of prospects are a better fit for a twelve-month short-term medical plan than for an ACA plan.

The Takeaway

☐ If you sell health insurance in your agency, consider adding short-term medical from a reputable carrier.

☐ Track the number of people you turned away last year and calculate the possible revenue gain by testing out another method.

☐ Test out a short-term medical product with one of your reps and calculate the revenue impact.

☐ If the revenue impact is significant, roll it out to the rest of the agency.

CHAPTER 17

The Simple Headshot Tweak That Instantly Makes You a Celebrity Agent

> *"Try not to become a person of success,*
> *but try to become a person of value."*
> —Albert Einstein

Application: B2B, B2C
Difficulty: Moderate
Time to implement: One week to three months
Cost to implement: Free to several thousand dollars

We work in one of the most regulated industries on the planet. Because of all the oversight, it can be very difficult to stand out. As a result, there's a bit of an identity crisis going on in the insurance world.

The Pershing Institute did a study in which they interviewed the top investors, as identified by *Fortune* magazine. Then, they reviewed the top advisors serving that level of investor.

The study found that consumers want an advisor who:

- Tailors his or her solutions to meet individual needs
- Works in the consumer's best interest
- Has experience

Why Your Prospects Think You're the Same as the Other Guy

The good news is that the leading financial advisors Pershing studied were indeed highlighting similar value propositions on their websites.

Unfortunately, virtually all of the advisors highlighted these values . . . and little else.

This means that the only thing the advisors were telling their clients was that they "tailor their solutions," "work in their clients' best interest," and are "experienced investment managers."

They *thought* they were setting themselves apart.

But really, they all still looked the same!

Here's the truly crushing part.

According to the study, 60 percent — more than half — of all investors cannot distinguish among advisors at all!

That's a shame.

Because if you're reading this book, you are one of a special breed of advisors and agents who really feels that you have something unique to offer. You're reading this book to learn specific strategies and techniques that will help separate you from every other agent out there.

Which brings us to the question:

How can you position yourself as a market authority and dramatically improve your results, sales, and deal flow?

Brand Exposure Leads to Brand Trust and Allegiance

To really understand the situation, I want to share a bit of neuroscience with you.

Back in 2002, a study showed that the more attention a product receives, the more likely consumers will be to choose it. This is VERY important to understand if you're going to make the *SHIFT* to become a desired authority in your field.

Traditionally, the way companies approach this is by raising a large budget and doing lots of marketing, so that they are seen most often and remembered best.

That's what billion-dollar companies such as The Coca-Cola Company, PepsiCo., Apple Inc., and Nike Inc. do every day. They figure that the more you and I see LeBron James, Serena Williams, or Brett Favre with a product, the more likely we will be to choose that product.

Advertisers know that celebrity endorsements are a powerful way to get us to pay attention, because the celebrity already has authority in our minds. Looking good, Brett!

These companies don't have to deliver value in their ads. Their ads don't have to lead directly to a conversation or a sale. They know you're going to see their ad ten-plus times over the course of a month and they trust that this repetition will lead you to buy their product.

It works.

Brand Exposure Makes a Brand Seem Better Than It Is

But another interesting study done in 1998, and again in 2000, examined something neuroscientists call "processing fluency." (Reber et al., 1998, Winkielman et al., 2000)

Processing fluency is a science that suggests that <u>items that come to mind more quickly will be liked better and will appear to be of higher value.</u>

So, your product doesn't necessarily have to *be* of a higher value — people just have to think it is. And they will, <u>if it a) remains top-of-mind; or b) is associated with media, logos, or brands that — or people who — ALREADY HAVE authority or value in their minds.</u>

How to Use This Data with No Marketing Budget at All

That's good news for those of us with a small budget. It means we just have to associate ourselves with brands that people already love, leverage those brands to attract consumer attention, and use those brands in our marketing.

Add One Little Line to Your Business Card

Let me give you an example of how this can be done.

You're probably a member of one or several trade associations. Picture your business card. Wouldn't it have more impact with one of those association logos on it (with permission, naturally)?

Of course it would.

Now, imagine this on your card: "As seen on CNN.com."

Can you see how that would boost not only your confidence, but also your potential clients' confidence in you? It would probably send both through the roof.

Actually, I know it would, because I measured it. I personally ran a test where I included my major media citations on my LinkedIn profile — right on my picture. I included that I was cited on CNN (which I was).

In fewer than thirty days, there was a 314 percent increase in the number of people who clicked on my profile — just because of that little logo.

A screenshot of my LinkedIn profile's increase in views over a thirty-day window after adding my media mentions to my headshot.

Add a Big Brand Logo and Change Everything

This is Terry.

Terry is a hardworking agent based in California.

He recently saved a small town more than $26,000 in benefit costs with his creative strategies. Do you think Terry is worth $500 an hour?

Ninety percent of people will say "no" — just based on his picture.

Now, let me show you a different image.

This is the same Terry who saved a small town $26,000 in benefit costs.

And he's been mentioned on CNN.

Is *this* agent worth $500 an hour?

Whenever I pose this question to a roomful of people, 80 percent inevitably change their mind right then and there. They give him a raise out of thin air!

All we did was make one small change to his photo.

Your Prospects Are Hardwired to Recognize Major Brands

Imagine for a moment how many billions of impressions have been made on your mind since childhood.

In a university study called "Too Young to Read, Old Enough to Shop," logos for McDonald's, Disney, and Toyota were shown to children aged three to five who couldn't yet read.

They immediately knew what each one was.

They knew that McDonald's was fast-food, Disney was Mickey Mouse, and Toyota was cars.

If branding has that much impact on the mind of a five-year-old, can you imagine how much it affects *you*?

That's why, when you saw Terry's photo attached to a small, familiar logo just a few centimeters wide, you immediately changed your opinion about him. The visual cortex of your brain shuffled through your memories and decided whether you trusted him.

When that logo was there, you trusted him more because you've learned to trust the logo.

When a financial advisor client of mine used these brands on her seminar invites, her attendees soared 128 percent over previous campaigns!

How to Tweak Your Website to Convert More Leads

Your goal is to turn as much of your traffic into leads as possible, right? So why not use this technique on your own website?

Let's do an experiment.

Look at this simple website. It's for Tracey Booker, a thirty-one-year-old financial planner who does fee-based financial planning.

Just based on the layout, would you pay her $2500 for a comprehensive financial plan?

When I ask this question in my talks, most people say "no."

But now look at the same website after I've made a slight adjustment.

Now, let me ask you the same question: Just based on the layout, would you pay her $2,500 for a comprehensive financial plan?

In most rooms, about 80 percent of the audience turns around and says "yes."

You feel more confident about her expertise this time, right? Yet, the design of the site didn't change at all. The ONLY change was adding the media citations.

Now, the Real Stuff: How to Get Featured in the Media

So how can you go about getting yourself featured in media in the first place?

Help a Reporter Out (HARO)

First, sign up for Help a Reporter Out (helpareporter.com).

HARO is a global network of tens of thousands of reporters looking for sources every single day. When they're working on a story, HARO is one of the first places they go.

HARO's e-mail newsletter goes out to hundreds of thousands of people. It contains all of the top stories being covered and reporters looking for sources.

You can help them out with stories about life insurance, annuities, financial services, etc. All you need is a great angle and a great pitch.

The Early-Morning TV-Show Pitch

Another ninja strategy is to call television stations in your area at around four o'clock in the morning. Ask to speak to a producer and offer to come on as a guest to talk about some local trends.

Be sure that when you call with your pitch, you tie your story in with actual trends.

But what stories are "hot"? You can find out by searching Google for trends in your industry. Trade publications are another great source of trends. As you pitch, mention the trend; then mention how you can provide advice on it.

Hire a Consultant—but Be Careful

Or, you can hire somebody to do it for you. Over on elance.com, you can hire a public-relations consultant on retainer for anywhere from $2,500 to $10,000 a month.

Now, here's a shameless plug:

I've personally gone through the media wheelhouse many, many times. In seven years, I spent well over half a million dollars on media buying.

Unfortunately, not a single one of the media or PR consultants I hired was able to get me on television. This was a huge disappointment, not only to me, but also to my clients.

So, I went out and started my own boutique PR consulting firm, *where clients pay only when they get coverage.*

So far, we've placed more than 237 agents, financial advisors, professionals, lawyers, and doctors in such prestigious outlets as Forbes, Fortune, Oprah Winfrey, Dr. Phil, Dr. Oz, Rachel Ray, Bloomberg, CNN Financial, HGTV, Conan O'Brien, over fifty local news stations, and all the regional news stations.

We've gotten clients cited in prestigious digital publications such as Business Insider, The Huffington Post, forbes.com, CNN.com, and many more.

If you would like more media exposure on a pay-for-performance basis, just contact my office. Everybody reading this book will get a 10 percent discount on even our premium-level service — a deal worth thousands of dollars. Start the process at www. GuaranteedMediaServices.com.

We now return you to your regularly scheduled book reading!

Summary

Overwhelming scientific and real-world evidence suggests that people make decisions on your value as an advisor or agent based on how FAST they can associate you with something they like.

If you don't have a large marketing or PR budget, the best way to take advantage of that fact is to leverage brands or media outlets that your clients already value. By doing so, you gain "instant authority" in their minds.

The Takeaway

- ☐ Add any association logos you have permission to use to your profile picture, website, and business card.
- ☐ Use helpareporter.com to contact journalists looking for sources, pitch a timely story to your local TV news station, or hire a consultant to help you get media placements.
- ☐ Anytime you're covered in the media, add that information to your LinkedIn profile.
- ☐ Include your most prestigious citations as small logos on your photo.
- ☐ Use that photo on LinkedIn, Facebook, and anywhere your prospects might see you.
- ☐ Contact www.GuaranteedMediaServices.com to get you in the media.

CHAPTER 18

Incredible Introductions: Using Education and Content to Approach Prospects as a "Business Growth Expert"

"There's no such thing as a long piece of work,
except one that you dare not start."
—Charles Baudelaire

Application: B2B, B2C
Difficulty: Advanced
Time to implement: One to six months
Cost to implement: Varies

One of the most common complaints I hear from insurance agents and financial advisors is how hard it is to get an appointment with the decision-maker.

Sam had this problem when he came to me. He was stuck in a six-month rut where he wasn't seeing any new clients. His referrals had dried up. He had no thought leadership in place that could generate a constant flow of leads.

When he joined my Platinum membership program, I helped him develop a specific strategy called "Incredible Introductions."

An Incredible Introduction positions you as an extremely valuable resource from the moment you meet your ideal prospect. My philosophy is this: since there are many ways to be introduced to somebody, why choose to be introduced at the common level when you can be introduced in a preeminent manner?

What you want to do is engineer an introduction that positions you as an authority, someone who everybody wants to do business with. That's what Sam had never done. He had always been "just another insurance agent."

But that was all about to change.

Promote Your Expertise

I asked Sam to put himself in his prospect's shoes, to ask himself, "What MAJOR business challenges are MY IDEAL prospects facing right now?"

The key to being an authority is not to limit yourself by what YOU know. You don't need to know how to solve every problem; you just need to be able to find somebody who can.

Let's get back to Sam's inspiring example.

What I did was teach Sam one of my advanced prospecting strategies: using LinkedIn to gain access to C-suite prospects. This strategy is a combination of using advanced searching, using the paid Sales Navigator feature and an outsourced method of group building.

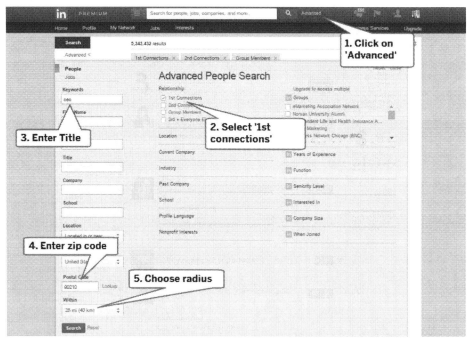

Using the "Advanced Search" feature of LinkedIn, you can find a desired market like CFOs of companies over fifty employees in a specific geography. Once you connect with them, you can send them a series of well-written e-mail messages that get opened and receive a response.

This is area where, with 90 percent certainty, you can land one new appointment a week with a desirable CEO, CMO, CFO, or other executive. In other words, setting up "Incredible Introductions."

Many of my clients are doing over twenty appointments a month using this strategy, in a completely outsourced method.

In addition to using this strategy to gain leads for himself, Sam started to hold intimate lunch workshops where he would teach his target audience of CEOs, CMOs, and CFOs how to do this themselves — how to grow their OWN businesses using LinkedIn.

Are you seeing the connection here?

With an "Incredible Introduction," the prospect got to know Sam as a Business Growth Agent — not just another financial advisor or insurance agent. Sam had created an incredibly direct path right to the prospect.

For Sam, it was much easier to get in the door to talk about business growth strategies than to sell financial services or insurance programs. With this new approach, doors were opening doors for him that previously had been closed. His profits have exploded as a result — and yours can too.

You can introduce yourself as an insurance agent or financial advisor . . . or you can get an "Incredible Introduction" by a local thought leader, connection, and business growth strategist.

What ideas have you encountered in this book so far around which you could create small workshops?

Write a few down here:

Workshop Idea #1: _____

Workshop Idea #2: _____

Workshop Idea #3: _____

Connecting Clients with Outside Experts

How can you apply this strategy in your market?

Say you're going after contractors who happen to be having a hard time growing their businesses. Find a local Facebook marketing expert and host a webinar on how contractors can grow their businesses.

You can call it "Facebook Marketing for Contractors," or "Facebook Marketing for Attorneys." Just name the training according to whom you want to attract to the class.

To make it a win-win situation, you can pay the expert for his time (though I have found that many will appear for free in the hope of getting a new client). Or, you can make him a consulting member of your organization and add him to your website as an unpaid staff member.

Then you market that class as a local live or virtual event, and invite only your desired audience.

They're easy enough to find if you know where to look and what to do:

- LinkedIn groups for your desired audience
- Sponsored posts inside LinkedIn so your invitations show up in their stream
- Join a local chapter of their association and host a class
- Place ads in industry publications
- Use SRDS.com to locate lists of businesses and professions by SIC code

The possibilities to help your market are all around you.

But you must SHIFT your thinking toward developing solutions OUTSIDE of your normal sales focus. Only in this way can you truly get "Incredible Introductions."

*SHIFT*ing to the Sale

Let's take this example of a local Facebook training a bit further, shall we?

Think of the longer-term impact of these kinds of seminars. In order for prospects to access the knowledge you are offering them, they must keep coming back to you.

They become accustomed to speaking with you on the phone and seeing you at the small workshops, so a relationship between you is developing.

When they ask you, "So where do I find the budget to try these cool things you're suggesting to me on Facebook?" it's a natural segue, when talking about funding the Facebook campaign, to say,

> *Well, let's take a look at your workers' comp and see if there are any discounts that could save you money that you could put toward your Facebook campaign.*

Brilliant!

There are many ways you can spin this for other verticals.

- A Medicare advisor who specializes in senior products hosts monthly health and vitality workshops for people over fifty-five and invites fitness and nutrition experts to present.
- A financial planner who targets seniors hosts "brain-games night" and invites the local senior community to come and play games that enhance their brain, giving open access to his desired audience, without expensive dinner seminars.

- A group benefits advisor hosts lunch-and-learns on how to market in down times.
- A financial advisor hosts a classic-car rally in the parking lot of a local restaurant, attracting investors.
- A high-end personal-lines agent books a local art gallery for an evening and hosts a wine-and-cocktail event centered around art for the affluent.
- One very successful (and enterprising) marketer sponsors a table at horse auctions where the target demographic is affluent men, his ideal clients.

The possibilities are endless. It's just a matter of thinking creatively and identifying your target audience's needs so that you can be there to serve them.

What could you offer your target audience that would benefit them? Who can you find who might know how to deliver that thought leadership or training?

Summary

Using Incredible Introductions can lead you to gain superior access to your desired market, no matter what market you sell to. You don't have to be the expert; you can simply be the conduit to helping your audience get a result they'll value.

This strategy may take a few months to get off the ground, but it can help you build a powerful group of local allies and prospects that will feed your pipeline for years to come.

The Takeaway 👍

☐ Think about your target market's specific needs.

☐ Hold a webinar or seminar around solving their problems.

☐ If you aren't qualified to present the information, team up with an expert who is.

☐ Use the introduction to segue into a sale.

CHAPTER 19

Incredible Introductions Part Two: "Would You Like to Be on My Radio Show?"

*"You can't put a limit on anything.
The more you dream, the farther you get."*
—Michael Phelps

Application: B2B
Difficulty: Moderate
Time to implement: Thirty minutes a day for two months
Cost to implement: Free to $100 a month

When Michael came to me, he was just getting started as an advisor and had no contacts in his desired market. So we worked together to create a campaign I'm going to outline to you in detail in this chapter. In the process, you'll learn one of my most coveted strategies, because it has a near 100 percent success rate, is easy to implement, and gives you incredible market advantage.

If you target high-profile clients and are looking for a long-term strategy that never gets old, you'll love this. It's a hybrid model used by Rick Liuag on the radio, but works just as effectively for a fraction of the cost. We'll talk about more on Rick's model in the following chapter ("How to Get Stellar Leads from Your Own Radio Show").

Welcome to Incredible Introductions, Part 2.

First, Find Your Target Prospects on LinkedIn

As Michael was familiar with my methods from LinkedIn, we decided to start there in developing his outreach methodology. What's nice about LinkedIn is you can directly target influencers you would like to have as clients.

For example, you can look for CEOs in New York. Or contractors in Illinois. Or HR managers in Colorado.

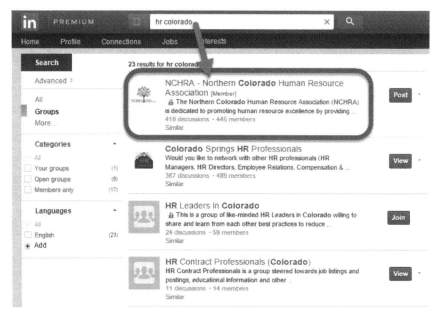

When you use the "Group Search" feature of LinkedIn, you will find a list of groups where your ideal target audience has gathered. Use the "Join" button to join the group.

If you're targeting just one city, use that instead of the state. For example: HR managers in Colorado.

You'll notice on the image here that you can click on the blue "Join" button. Most groups are "open" groups, in that anyone can join them. If there's a little lock symbol next to it, that means it's a "closed" group. You can still apply, but your acceptance won't be immediate.

One strategy we like to use for closed groups that don't let you in after a week is the following:

Send the group owner a message through LinkedIn like this:

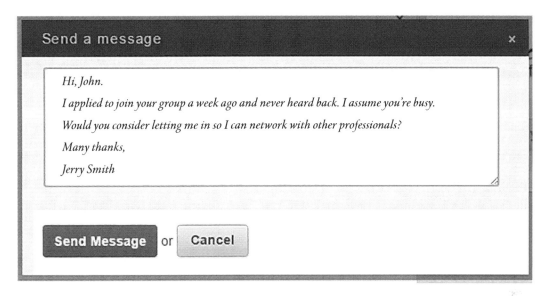

Ask Them to Speak on Your Radio Show

Once you're a part of the group, you can connect and message people directly in the network who are in your target audience.

I recommend connecting with around fifty a day. Any more than that with a free account and LinkedIn could pause your account. If you have a paid account, you can get away with fifty to eighty a day.

Once connected, you can send each of them a carefully scripted message on LinkedIn, such as:

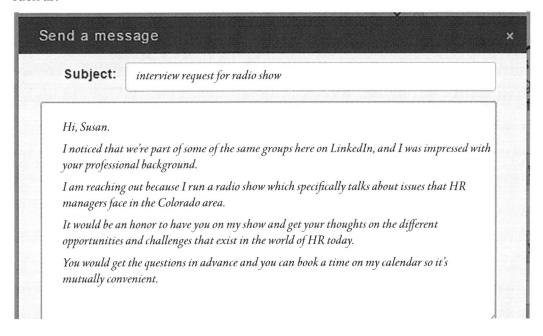

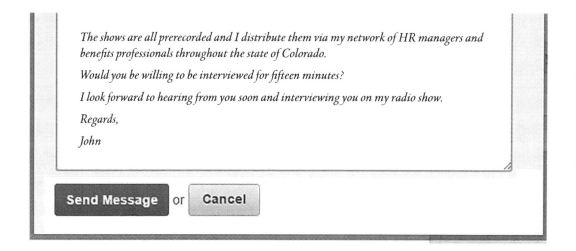

The shows are all prerecorded and I distribute them via my network of HR managers and benefits professionals throughout the state of Colorado.

Would you be willing to be interviewed for fifteen minutes?

I look forward to hearing from you soon and interviewing you on my radio show.

Regards,

John

Send Message or Cancel

It's so powerful to reach out to somebody this way — not as an agent, but as a . . . radio host! Imagine what identifying yourself as a prestigious radio host could do to your outreach efforts!

This is truly an Incredible Introduction because it *SHIFT*s you to a level that most agents will never reach. It makes you an established authority in your space.

OK, but . . . I Don't Have a Radio Show

At this point, you're probably wondering, well, how do I start a radio show?

Blogtalkradio.com is a good way to get started. It's how we got Michael set up with a show. He targeted CFOs in NYC and launched his show with a few connections he had made along the way, and within two weeks, he had two segments already recorded!

You don't need to overthink this or make it too complicated. You might even consider doing a podcast instead. I know of one woman who targets independent medical practices. She records a webinar on GoToWebinar, then turns it into a YouTube video, and finally, she turns the YouTube video into an iTunes podcast.

At this point, she has one thousand independent medical practitioners who listen to her podcast every month.

Brilliant.

Why This Works

Here's why this is such a good strategy. Having heard your show, the HR manager (or whoever your desired target might be) will want to know more about you. This is the perfect opportunity to talk about the various strategies and techniques you use to help other HR managers in your area.

Remember: The goal is to always be seen as THE preeminent expert in your space. If you can avoid it, NEVER be introduced as just another "agent" or "advisor."

And that's why this Incredible Introduction is so powerful.

As of the writing of this book, using this technique and my advanced LinkedIn strategies, Michael was consistently connecting with several hundred NEW CFOs in NYC every week — and booking a minimum of one new prospect meeting.

Summary

You've just learned a powerful approach to building your brand and getting difficult-to-reach prospects on the phone, using a high-level approach most advisors don't know about.

Approaching prospects as an industry authority who hosts a radio show on issues and opportunities within that space takes you out of the "insurance agent" box and puts you in the coveted "industry expert" category.

You don't need a large budget to make this work, either. An account with blogtalkradio — which costs just a few dollars a month — and a phone are all you need to get started today.

How much might your response rate grow today by putting this methodology in place? How many additional opportunities to speak to your desired target audience might you have by using this technique?

The Takeaway

☐ Use Blogtalkradio to create a radio show.

☐ Introduce yourself to professionals in your target market by asking them to speak on your show.

☐ Leverage that opportunity to connect with them and earn their business.

CHAPTER 20

How to Get Stellar Leads from Your Own Radio Show

"Don't try to be better than the next advisor.
Try to be better than the advisor you were yesterday."
—Jeremiah Desmarais

Application: B2B
Difficulty: Moderate
Time to implement: Two to six hours
Cost to implement: $99 a month

Did anyone ever tell you that you have "a face for radio"?

If so, you should be grateful, my friend. Radio marketing can be a powerful and lucrative method for building market authority and preeminence for an insurance or financial advisor. Even in this digital age.

According to a 2013 study, a whopping 91 percent of Americans aged twelve and over listen to AM/FM radio every single week. This is higher than the number of Americans who use Facebook. And these people don't just tune in for a song or two. The share of total hours Americans spend listening to terrestrial radio, compared to their time on the Internet and satellite, is a whopping 81 percent.

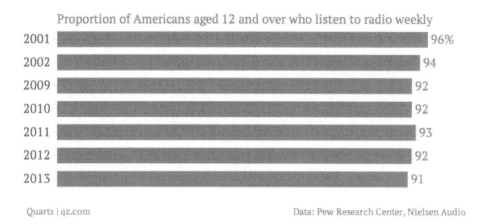

Proportion of Americans aged 12 and over who listen to radio weekly

Year	Percentage
2001	96%
2002	94
2009	92
2010	92
2011	93
2012	92
2013	91

Quartz | qz.com   Data: Pew Research Center, Nielsen Audio

When you consider how much time is spent in the car, it makes sense. As much as 44 percent of all radio listening takes place in the car, where AM/FM radio has an 80 percent share, according to Macquarie Capital (April 2014).

In this chapter, we'll review a powerful strategy used by a financial advisor and benefits expert who's using radio to carve an incredible market share in one of the most competitive markets in the country.

"They Are Actually Happy That You've Called"

Rick Liuag is a long-time health insurance agent who got into financial planning years ago. As a result, he's very familiar with both the health insurance side of things and how to protect your money using life-insurance strategies.

He's the host of the Los Angeles show "Safe Money Radio," and says that his best financial leads come from his radio program.

When done right, radio broadcasting can help you gain your clients' attention and trust while building massive credibility in your audience's eyes.

Its benefits are augmented by the increased exposure of podcast replays.

"When someone hears you on the radio, and then you call them, their attitude toward you is totally different," says Rick. "It's almost as if they feel they know you. They are actually happy that you've called."

Double or Triple Your Closing Rate

Rick estimates that he *tripled* his closing rate just by investing in his radio show and podcast last year rather than purchasing leads traditionally.

Even high-quality purchased leads will net just a 10–20 percent closing rate, but by working with call-ins from his show, Rick's closing ratio has soared up to 60 percent. The incredible authority-building power of radio has helped him establish INSTANT credibility.

Rick has reaped the benefits of being a local celebrity, and is on track to close as many as *half* of his radio-show leads this year. He's also noticed that his callers tend to be well educated and affluent, with more income to protect.

Is Radio for You?

Radio and podcasting are not for everyone, though. "Depending on your geography, the costs of land radio can be very high," Rick says. "You have to make certain that you have room in your budget and you need to be positive that the station you've chosen reaches the right demographic for your particular strategies."

Craft a Compelling Message for Maximum Success

Rick also believes it's crucial to have a unique message. In today's attention-deficit world, advisors need an intriguing and unusual message to get good results in the media. Rick often uses Obamacare as a hook for his shows, emphasizing the potential threats that the Affordable Care Act poses to seniors on Medicare.

"This is a hot topic that really gets seniors to pay attention," he says.

What topic is so hot for your market right now that it might compel them to listen to you?

Spreading Your Message across the Globe

Liuag is in the process of building a podcast network where other advisors and agents will be able to post their own podcasts on various asset-production strategies and reach a worldwide audience.

In addition to maintaining a presence on AM/FM radio, Liuag broadcasts regularly on the BlogTalkRadio.com platform for just a few dollars a month. This is a great platform to get started on because it's inexpensive and simple. You can always build from there.

Liuag's BlogTalk page is well done, as you can see, and allows him to add a call to action that generates VERY low-cost leads for his services.

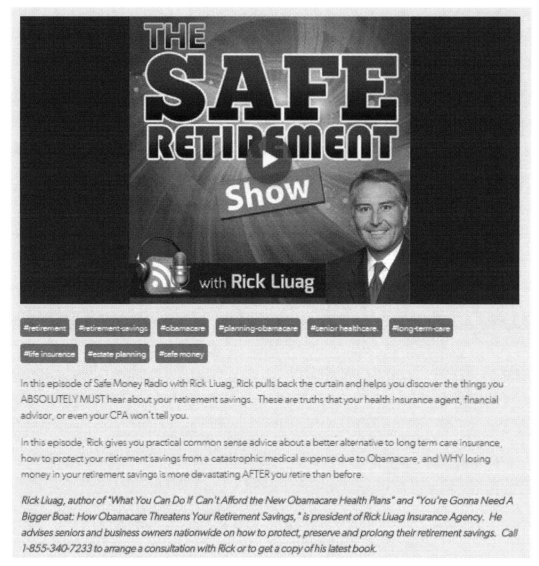

Rick promotes his book and a free consultation at the bottom of his streaming radio station on Blogtalkradio.com.

So How Much Will This Cost—and What's My Return?

Rick's show can be heard in Los Angeles, where airtime and production on a major station can be pricey – he estimates that he spends between $6,000 and $7,000 each month – but your costs will depend on where you live. In Austin, Texas, for example, a show like Liuag's would cost around $2,000 a month. Or, you can produce a professional podcast for less than $200 a month.

Rick says he gets an average of ten good leads per show, so if he puts out four shows a month, that's forty high-quality leads at roughly $162 per lead. With a close to 50 percent closing ratio, he's closing large cases for around $324 per acquisition. That is incredibly low for annuities! He's projected at least $250,000 in earnings over the next six months.

Twelve months of this kind of marketing costs him $72,000 a year — for a net PROFIT of $178,000 in first-year commissions, not to mention the residuals, referrals, speaking invitations, and other opportunities that will follow.

Keep in mind that Rick sells annuities, IUL, structured settlements, and other life products, and case sizes tend to be a bit higher in California. Still, Rick says the leads he generates are better than those from any other method he's tried — and more of them come from radio than from podcasting.

The end result? If you're a good closer, in Los Angeles, you can spend $40,000 and earn at least $100,000 gross.

If you'd like more help with the specifics, Tammy de Leeuw specializes in helping insurance advisors produce radio shows and podcasts. You can find her on LinkedIn.

Summary

In this chapter, we reviewed the unique market advantages of being on the radio. In addition to providing you with an exclusive platform to showcase your thought leadership, it drives qualified leads that can be highly lucrative.

While reserved for those who have a budget in excess of $5,000 a month for larger markets, radio generates higher-quality leads and closes at a higher rate than Internet-based leads do, where there's no previous connection.

If you're looking for market stature, high-quality leads, and a platform for your ideas, being on the radio could be a strong option for you.

What could you offer to radio listeners that would impact their lives and attract them to you? What impact would it have on your business over the course of one year, two years, five years to be on the radio?

The Takeaway 👍

- ☐ Research local stations and gather costs for a weekly one-hour show.

- ☐ Look into podcast networks or platforms where you can broadcast for free.

- ☐ Develop a unique and timely message — something with a hook that you come back to time and time again.

- ☐ Work the leads that come in from your show.

CHAPTER 21

How Social Networks Are Adding New Alternatives to Direct Marketing

"Consistently investigate what gives other people energy.
Be the fan that fuels it."
—Darren Rowse

Up to this chapter in the book, I've been sharing with you powerful distinctions, perspectives, and 360-degree "CAT scan-like" views of your market to help you generate more leads, appointments, and commissions.

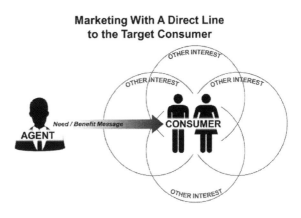

As we transition to more advanced digital concepts, I'd like to take a break from the ideas and share with you a perspective that could open your mind to the idea of using social media.

It comes from one of my long-time colleagues and collaborators, Tom Carolan. Tom was one of the co-founders of Parasol Leads, one of the country's highest ranked lead-generation companies, winner of the Best Leads Quality in America award from the LeadsCouncil.

For a long time, insurance professionals were told to identify their target market and then deliver their message directly to that market. This approach worked well through the 1990s, and even into the early 2000s. Insurance agents in business for twenty years or more probably remember how well this direct-line approach worked. The response rates. The appointment volume. The packed seminar rooms.

An Era of Disruptive Change

Then, all at once, the direct-line approach became much more difficult. First, we entered the era of financial-services deregulation and consolidation. And then, we saw the explosion of the Internet.

The Financial Services Modernization Act of 1999 — or the Gramm–Leach–Bliley Act — blurred the lines between life-insurance producers, investment advisors, mortgage advisors, and other such professionals. At the same time, the Internet delivered volumes of information to consumers quickly and easily. The perceived need for a human intermediary waned.

And when consumers did feel they needed help, they could get it from their bank, financial advisor, or other professional entity with whom they already had a relationship.

This all created a much more competitive landscape. The independent producer no longer had the upper hand. He became David to the Goliath of the big banks and financial-services firms.

That is, until now.

SHIFT Your Mindset from Direct to Indirect Marketing

The very innovation that put you at a disadvantage — the Internet — has evolved to give you the upper hand once again. You just have to look at marketing indirectly, rather than sticking with the old-fashioned direct approach.

Social media has leveled the playing field and, in many ways, put the large firm at a disadvantage. The key word is "social." Corporations are much less effective on social media than the individual producer. To the consumer, they seem less personal. More out of touch. Their message is corporate, and it's not relevant.

When done correctly, social media marketing gives you an indirect line to the consumer, and that line allows you to establish a relationship of trust.

You do this with a constant flow of small bits of information that interest the consumer.

Marketing with an Indirect Line to the Target Consumer

Often, this information is not directly related to your area of expertise. Instead, you deliver your message indirectly, over time.

Simply put, you are building both trust and recognition with the target consumer.

Winning with the Indirect Approach

When Tom started Parasol Leads, he used social media to market indirectly to consumers; then he followed up that effort with a CRM that analyzed interactions and identified additional opportunities. As a result, Parasol Leads won the Best Leads Quality in America award from the LeadsCouncil in January 2014.

Tom has since sold Parasol Leads, but his strategy stands are an example of how the Internet can be one of the most cost-effective sources of leads.

As we jump into the next section, keep in mind that you can use these "indirect/direct" strategies to complement your current marketing efforts.

Anyone who tells you that Internet marketing is the "end all" solution is either trying to sell you a program about that technique, or simply doesn't have the experience of generating over two million leads and hundreds of millions in sales, as I've had the privilege of doing for over one hundred thousand advisors in fifty-one countries.

CHAPTER 22

LinkedIn: You're Doing It Wrong (and How to Fix That)

"Social media is about connecting with customers in a meaningful way — a way the customer determines is meaningful."

—Duane Forrester

Application: B2B
Difficulty: Moderate
Time to implement: Twenty minutes a day
Cost to implement: Free

I was recently conducting a class for my higher-end "mastermind" clients, and was covering the topic of whether LinkedIn was a valuable place to spend time marketing. What's interesting was that in preparing for this call, one of my contacts at LinkedIn corporate headquarters shared with me a valuable white paper on the "state of the nation" for LinkedIn and the insurance space.

Though the statistics I quote from it here are specific to commercial insurance, I think you'll see that the concepts and trends we cover in this chapter apply to all verticals. You'll understand why in a moment.

The white paper is called *Commercial Insurance Today: How Rising Adoption of Digital and Social Resources Impacts Decision-Making.* In the author's report on a study he/she did of 477 commercial insurance clients and 297 commercial producers, all LinkedIn members based in the U.S.

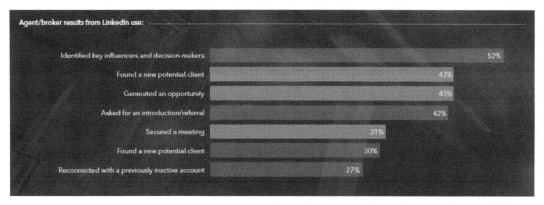

Source: LinkedIn

(NOTE: Regardless of the kind of insurance or financial services you sell, the data is highly relevant to you as well. The only markets this is not applicable to are Medicare, Medicaid, LTC, and perhaps death-benefit plans.)

The clients were either decision-makers or key influencers within the fields of commercial insurance and employee benefits. The producers were independent or captive agents and brokers selling at least one line of commercial insurance or employee benefits.

What caught my eye is how brokers responded to the question of how they're using LinkedIn today. The responses fell into five main categories, in order of importance:

1. Listing credentials
2. Staying abreast of companies and executive changes
3. Conducting due diligence on potential clients
4. Identifying prospects
5. Staying up to date on risks relevant to carriers and clients

What's wrong with this list?

If you ask me, it's completely backwards.

"Identifying prospects" should be number one! But it's buried down there at number four! No wonder so many advisors are lost when attempting to use this powerful social networking tool: most are using it in the wrong way!

Turn Your Priorities around and Start Serving Your Prospects

Next, the study asked insurance CLIENTS how *they* use LinkedIn.

Here's what they said, in order of importance:

1. Looking for commentary or perspective on industry topics
2. Evaluating brokers or agents
3. Identifying prospective brokers or agents to work with
4. Staying up to date with company risks/learning about emerging liabilities
5. Researching insurance policies and products

This was a real eye-opener for me, and it probably is for you too, dear reader. Your clients are doing more than looking at your profile; **they are seeking <u>new perspectives and relevant commentary.</u>**

Three of my clients are currently using my LinkedIn approach (which follows) to lock in consistent business.

- Wilson and Company out of St. Louis, which offers a revolutionary new style of employee benefits for self-funded plans, is sharing valuable content and connecting with key decision-makers.
- Peter, a financial advisor from California who does executive-level compensation plans and creates golden handcuffs for start-ups, has generated over one hundred C-suite leads using this approach.
- Meridian out of New York, which focuses on the C-suite and developing personal-lines clients in the affluent market, has an agent with a backlog of thirty leads who want to do business with her because of her expertise.

The point is, if you don't contribute compelling commentary to LinkedIn, somebody else will.

It's simple to start.

Step 1: Join groups that have your target audience in them.

Step 2: Every week, post a great article for the group and ask for feedback.

Step 3: Post any articles, blog posts, webinars, and whitepapers produced by your firm as "helpful advice." Consider posting them to the Pulse network for added exposure.

Step 4: Invite your target audience to come and view your article and get their opinion. This is the LONGEST step to complete, but the most important! Getting relevant traffic and interaction with your prospects is the KEY!

One of my Platinum-level clients is sharing relevant articles with CFOs in the über-competitive New York City marketplace. He's getting one new appointment every single week doing this — without ever asking for a sale.

In one case, the CFO not only asked him to come in and look at their commercial-lines policy, but also offered him the chance to take over a three-thousand-member association of high-net-worth executives. The CFO didn't have time to run it himself — and because of my client's LinkedIn skill, he got a golden opportunity he can mine until he retires.

Offer your voice to the marketplace. Your target market is listening for it.

Check the credentials of a prospective broker or agent.

This same study I cited above revealed that 23 percent of the sample had chosen an agent or broker because of what they found on LinkedIn. That's nearly a *quarter* of all people interviewed!

And 42 percent said they would *increase* their use of networks such as LinkedIn and SlideShare over the next twelve months.

This should be a wake-up call for you.

If your LinkedIn profile is outdated, shoddy, or incomplete, bring it up to speed. You can do this by adding as much relevant content as possible: slideshows, articles, videos, photographs of you doing what you do best; the sky's the limit.

Use the new Projects section to highlight your recent successes.

LinkedIn has a great feature that most people never take advantage of: the Projects section. Here, you can add just about anything you've been working on to help boost your profile.

- Did you sign a new client? Post it!
- Did you get invited to speak at an event to share your thought leadership? Post it!
- Did you sign on with a new carrier? Post it!
- Did you hit a new personal best in your pull-ups? Post that, bad boy!

OK . . . all except for that last one are worthy of posting!

The Project section prompts you to list projects you've worked on — and that's pretty open-ended. It can mean clients. And metrics. To take advantage of this, list five clients you've helped in big ways. Include details.

Here's an example. Earlier this year, I was a keynote speaker at the Social Media Summit. I added that to my profile. It's not really a job, right? It's a project. But I can use it to enhance my credibility. And it only took me a minute to put it up there.

When you do this, you'll be in the top 1 percent of 1 percent. Because if you look at most agent profiles, you get a basic CV and nothing else.

Projects

Keynote Speaker - Social Media Summit Chicago

May 2015

Delivered Keynote address to 300 experts in Social Media at the Chicago Social Media Summit.

Other notable speakers were Heidi Barker Sa Shekhem, McDonalds; Gina Ballenger, Twitter; Josh Weaver, Zappos.

Interviewed as Webinar Marketing Thought Leader on International Product Launch

April 2015

Was selected to be one of 10 Top Experts in business growth and strategy to share how to create high converting webinars that build brands, sales and profits. Shared case study on how one webinar we designed generated $98,400 in just 90 minutes.

Watch the video here: https://www.youtube.com/watch?t=1429&v=pz81N92HscA

How I use speaking engagements on my profile to stand out at
https://www.linkedin.com/in/jeremiahdesmarais. Feel free to connect with me there.
I'm an "Open Networker" and accept all invitations.

Identify prospective brokers and agents to work with.

So, your ideal clients are on LinkedIn, looking for you and your expertise. Period.

If you're not actively using LinkedIn as a prospecting tool and keeping your profile up to date, you're missing a huge opportunity — and leaving the window wide open for your competition to jump in.

If you write an article or a blog post, put it on your profile. Include it in your status update. Post it in a group and start a discussion around it. Same goes for podcasts or webinars. Have your recording transcribed and throw it up there.

Give your target market what they want.

Research insurance policies or products.

Remember that your audience is going to LinkedIn to learn more about insurance policies and products. This offers a great opportunity, but don't squander it by selling. Instead of talking about policies and products, talk about *risk*.

For example: Michael is really into cyber liability. That would be a great topic to discuss on LinkedIn. Data breaches, data theft, mitigating risk, etc. It plays right into what their target markets want: information on risk and liabilities and information on policies and products that help mitigate that risk.

There's no question that agents and brokers are on LinkedIn. Nine out of ten agents rely on professional networks to build their business, and three-fifths of them plan to increase their reliance on such networks. What's more, **forty-three percent of commercial insurance professionals have found a new client on LinkedIn.**

You're already there. Now it's time to *SHIFT* your approach.

Summary

There's no hiding from it; LinkedIn is a powerful social media network you can use to reach your desired audience in the B2B world. The data is clear and speaking loudly! Your prospects are spending HOURS researching the products and services you sell.

Instead of using LinkedIn just as a social network where you can post your profile, use techniques such as group posting, project updating, and profile boosting to get the upper hand in your market.

What could you post on your profile today that will help set you apart from the other advisors in your area? What valuable piece of content is on your hard drive right now that you could share with your ideal market?

The Takeaway 👍

☐ Start or join group groups where your prospects are.

☐ Share relevant content to spark interesting conversations and invite your core audience to comment on it. Ask, "What do you think of this article?"

☐ Update, complete, and optimize your profile.

☐ Use the new Project section to list clients, metrics, and other one-off accomplishments.

CHAPTER 23

Using Simple Strategies to Target Tribes of Prospects

"It is not necessary to do extraordinary things to get extraordinary results."
—Warren Buffet

Application: B2B, B2C
Difficulty: Moderate
Time to implement: One week to three months
Cost to implement: Free to several thousand dollars

OK, Marketing Master in the Making, up until now you've been learning about what many of my clients and students do to find individuals in the market. We've covered e-mail marketing, Facebook, YouTube, direct response, and other things.

I hope by now your mind is abuzz with the market potential you have in front of you right now. But before we continue with more hard-hitting examples you can swipe and deploy, I wouldn't be doing my duty if I didn't share with you a powerful way to grow your prospect base: targeting tribes.

In this chapter, you'll come to understand a powerful distinction that can help you laser focus your marketing efforts in an area where GROUPS of dozens, hundreds, or even thousands of your ideal markets are spending time.

If you can understand and appreciate this point, you'll be on your way to dominating your market and investing your marketing dollars wisely. The result will be windfall profits for years to come.

Marketing to Tribes

Targeting tribes is a three-step process:

Step 1: Identify your ideal market. This could be doctors, lawyers, recently divorced widows, pre-retirees with a net worth of over half a million dollars, CEOs, CFOs, HR directors, etc.

Step 2: Research what interests this market, other than what is normally governed by age, title, or insurance type. For example, many wealthy people are into horses, so online equestrian clubs could be a good place for prospecting.

Step 3: Find a way to sponsor, promote, or participate in these organizations or groups. As an idea, one financial advisor sponsors fancy wine tastings for auto clubs. As a result, he has a captive market of high-net-worth car collectors who see him first through a social lens, then a professional one — which increases his brand and positioning.

The Jeweler Who Loves Horses

One jeweler who's targeting the same market as most financial advisors is really into horses and goes to a lot of equine auctions. He's like the rest of the guys there: male, affluent, and married.

He knows that when one of them goes home with a $15,000 horse, his wife may be a bit upset. But if he also shows up with a nice piece of jewelry, that might ease the tension and keep the marriage happy. So he sets up a booth at these shows and helps his fellow horse aficionados pick out baubles to appease their wives.

Taking the Networking Strategy Online

By the way, you can adapt this approach for use online, as well. LinkedIn and other networking sites are rife with groups focused on specific interests.

There are groups on LinkedIn centered on many professional titles as well as social interests. Here are a few examples:

- CXO Group (for CEOs, CFOs, CIOs, CMOs, and more): 135,737 members
- Human Resources (HR) and Talent Management Executives: 383,112 members
- Equestrian Professionals: 5,926 members
- Hunting, Fishing, and Outdoor Professionals: 9,850 members
- US Lacrosse Members: 8,554 members

Join some of these groups (it's free!), and by means of an introduction to what you do, offer to send your fellow members a special PDF report to help them with a problem related to the group.

If you're in an equestrian group, for instance, offer a list of the top horse trainers in the area. If it's about lacrosse, maybe you can help by sharing some playing tips for their kids. All of this is easily searchable via Google, even if you don't have expertise in the area.

One of my clients is deeply into lacrosse and is using one of my advanced LinkedIn strategies to target fellow fans for large commercial-lines deals.

Another client is landing an appointment with a CFO every week by using one of my advanced techniques.* He posts relevant content to his targeted LinkedIn groups and, as a result, he caught the eye of a founder of a New York biotech organization that recently named him the COO of the organization! Now he has direct access to more than two hundred of his ideal clients.

Yet another advisor has designed evenings in which he engages seniors in brain games, weaving a brief commercial for his services throughout the evening. He's completely stopped doing investment seminars and, just a few years ago, made several million dollars in commissions using these techniques.

*If you're interested in learning more about my advanced targeting strategies, including those utilizing LinkedIn, please contact my office. We also have a "Done for You" service that guarantees twenty meetings a month through LinkedIn.

Summary

Targeting tribes can be a powerful way to increase your profits and market effectiveness. By carefully doing your research and looking for ways to provide value to your audience, you can own exclusive niches that most advisors and agents will never find.

What market segments are waiting for a creative thinker like you to come in and help them by offering value? Where could you go where your ideal audience is spending time right now, where your competitors aren't?

The Takeaway 👍

- ☐ Go online and search for your target market: _____ conference or _____ trade show (for instance, "construction conference" or "construction trade show").
- ☐ Attend the events that make sense for your market and your budget.
- ☐ Network with the professionals at these events, on their level.
- ☐ Brainstorm a list of ideas using this chapter to inspire ways you can participate, present, or sponsor content.

CHAPTER 24

How to Build a Seven-Figure Virtual Agency with Pay-Per-Click Campaigns

"If you do what you've always done, you'll get what you've always gotten."
—Tony Robbins

Application:
B2B,
B2C
Difficulty: Advanced
Time to implement: Three hours to start, then one hour per day
Cost to implement: $10 to $20 per day

It can be hard to know where to start sometimes. There are so many options and apps, it's hard to keep track of it all. You go to a seminar and hear an agent spew out a few apps or tools he's using, you write it all down furiously, and you get back to the office all jazzed.

You go back to your notes, invigorated with the ideas and ready to implement. *This is going to be the day! you say to yourself. It's all going to change now!*

Then reality sets in.

Does this app go with my contact manager? How does it work with e-mail? Will I be able to use this font here?

And you get overwhelmed.

Sound familiar?

Trust me, I've been there dozens of times myself.

To look at the big picture, let's talk about an agent I've consulted with many times over the past two years. I love his story and I think you will too because it's a great example of how you can take simple tools and ideas from other markets and import them into yours.

You're going to hear about how a small one-man operation built one of the fastest-growing insurance operations in California and then sold it for seven figures, cash — just EIGHTEEN months later!

You'll discover the tools he used and the marketing system that fed his small, hungry team of agents. Along the way, I'll share with you exactly how you can duplicate this model, whether you're a one-person operation or a large, multi-advisor firm.

Note: Though this was a health- and life-insurance agency, the frameworks of virtual operations, digital marketing, and workflow are applicable to all verticals with just a little SHIFT in thinking.

The Birth of a Virtual Agency

When Sy Wemhaner came into the insurance industry in his thirties, he noticed that the agents around him were doing an awful lot of driving, going from one appointment to the next.

When he suggested there had to be a better way, they scoffed. "This is the way we've always done it," they said.

And to Sy, that sounded like a challenge.

Sy grew his agency by looking at what worked elsewhere — and what didn't. By taking a look at traditional agencies, he noticed they had great retention, but fewer sales. Virtual agencies and call centers had great sales but terrible retention, due to the common "boiler room" mentality to get the policy sold.

So, instead, he hired agents off (of all places) Craigslist to work his leads.

Craigslist may seem like an odd place to find agents, but you'd be amazed at the wide variety of people you can find there looking for a new gig.

Next, to keep his operation entirely virtual, he used a simple internet-based phone system such as Grasshopper, so his employees could be anywhere in the world and still answer the phone as if they were right down the hall. He bought a standard VoIP phone for every agent, at around $150 a pop.

And just like that, he built a network of agent employees around the country in fewer than thirty days.

Fast-forward a year-and-a-half later, when Sy sold the agency, they were averaging seventeen hundred policy sales a month, with twenty-one agents.

The entire monthly cost of operations? Four hundred dollars to run the whole thing.

No office space. No furniture. No commuting.

Because of this *SHIFT* in thinking and operations, Sy was outperforming huge brokers with $40 million worth of property and two hundred agents.

Could your agency benefit from using a VoIP service to create a professional image? What would it look like for you to move from your office to an entirely virtual operation? If you can't do it all at once, what about going virtual just one day a week to see how it works?

Generating Leads through Search Engine Marketing

Here's the part I love the most about Sy's strategy. He generated his *own* leads, but not the way you may be thinking.

Instead of relying on traditional lead companies, he started off with limited knowledge, generating leads through pay-per-click campaigns and search engine optimization (SEO).

Here's how he did it.

To create effective and cost-effective PPC ads, Sy focused on individual communities instead of statewide campaigns. For example, he knew that trying to bid on a term such as "Insurance in California" was a no-win. The competition is very high for that phrase and really only worth it for lead companies or carriers.

So he *SHIFT*ed his thinking. He thought small and bid on terms such as:

"Chula Vista Insurance."

"Victorville Insurance."

"Palo Alto Health Insurance."

By thinking of communities, he was able to get a click to his page for as low as a two to three dollars, rather than twenty to thirty.

Monitoring Results and Fine-Tuning for Success

Once the leads were coming in at the rate of a few a day, Sy closely monitored his agents' closing ratios. That's the next metric to pay close attention to.

What was key was that if they started closing less frequently, he assumed the problem was his leads — not the agents.

So he'd focus on a different area. Carrier rates can fluctuate month by month, so it's important for you to find out what areas your carrier is hot in, then get leads in those areas, where you'll have a better chance of quoting a competitive rate.

At any given time, Sy had five different ad campaigns going on.

By paying close attention to clicks and conversions, he could fine-tune his online marketing and lower his cost per lead and cost per acquisition.

Key Metrics for Successful PPC Campaigns

If you're about to venture into generating leads, here are a few helpful metrics to consider for your first campaign.

Sy estimated his average CPL (cost per lead) as follows:

- Health insurance: $18
- Life insurance: $29
- Small group: $41

From there, he calculated how many leads it would take to sell one policy (or his cost per acquisition). You can easily do this with a simple formula:

Number of leads generated before a sale is made X Cost per Lead =
Cost per Acquisition (CPA)
Example:
Ten leads at $10 a lead to close one deal = $100 cost per acquisition

Sy's CPA was:

- Health insurance: $90
- Life insurance: $130
- Small group: $200

These are good guidelines for you to use when planning your lead-generation efforts. We'll cover this in more detail in a later chapter.

A Secret Trick to Closing More Life-Insurance Leads

By staying on top of his numbers, Sy learned that he got a better return on investment by focusing on health insurance rather than life-insurance leads — even though he sold both.

For every ten health plans he sold, he was able to add on two-and-a-half life policies. But when he sold life as the primary, it took him eighteen sales to cross-sell one health plan.

By cross-selling life to his health clients, he lowered his CPA even more, because he could add the extra profit from the life-insurance sale to offset the cost of the lead being generated.

Since life already had a higher CPA on its own, he focused on health policies to maximize his efforts.

What's 61 Percent More Profitable: Google or Bing?

While most agents focus on Google AdWords when they want to start generating leads, Sy found that by advertising on the Bing/Yahoo! Platform, he was able to generate leads at a much lower cost without sacrificing quality. The reason came down to simple demographics.

Google tends to attract younger, more tech-savvy consumers under the age of thirty-five, while Bing users tend to be older, with families. The latter were within his demographic for selling health-insurance plans for families — and they were more likely to fill out a web form.

He also found that Bing generated more traffic for key insurance-related search terms. As a result, his clicks were 61 percent cheaper.

Which Is Better: Pay per Click or Search Engine Optimization?

Sy typically spent the same amount of money on PPC as on long-term SEO strategies.

About 20 percent of his revenue came from SEO. But that focus also required more time to manage: about 50 percent of his time. For that reason, if he were to do it again, he says, he would focus solely on PPC — and I would agree.

When you're starting out, there's always a risk that your efforts may not pay off with search engine optimization. Ever-changing search algorithms from Google can easily unseat weeks or months of effort.

But with a well-built PPC campaign, your returns are higher and more predictable, creating a kind of profit faucet. If you want more leads, you can turn the spigot to get more. When you want to relax, you can dial it down.

Summary

What you've just read is a great example of how, with a few *SHIFT*s in thinking, you can outgun even the biggest players with limited capital, resources, and staff.

Your office can be entirely virtual, and your clients will never know the difference.

You can run the entire operation for a few hundred dollars a month, using simple telephone- and web-based tools.

A steady stream of leads can feed your team if you implement low-cost, PPC campaigns on Bing to start off, then move to Google once you've gotten your metrics in place.

Hey, it's all up and running; you might be able to put your agency on the same path to success that my buddy Sy did — and sell it for seven figures in just eighteen months!

The Takeaway

- ☐ Consider using a VoIP service to help your operations go virtual.

- ☐ Test-drive a small budget of $100 toward a pay-per-click campaign on Bing, using targeted keywords that are community based.

- ☐ Keep track of analytics — specifically, cost per lead and cost per acquisition — and fine-tune your campaign as needed.

- ☐ Network with other like-minded Virtual agencies at www.Theshiftnation.org.

CHAPTER 25

How to Nurture Prospects Automatically with a High-Converting E-mail Strategy

> *"Patience, persistence, and perspiration make*
> *an unbeatable combination for success."*
> —Napoleon Hill

Application:
B2B, B2C
Difficulty: Moderate
Time to implement: Two hours
Cost to implement: $30 a month for software

Now that you have a video out there that's generating leads, what's the best way to use e-mail to follow up with your financial or insurance prospect?

Terry, a home and auto agent from Wisconsin, faced this dilemma. He was buying leads and was following up by phone only. He'd send the occasional e-mail out to the prospects, but "didn't want to be a nuisance," so he was careful not to be aggressive in his e-mail strategy.

The last thing Terry wanted to do is be that annoying agent who keeps calling and e-mailing until the prospect finally tells him to stop. So he did what 90 percent of agents and advisors do: he didn't follow up effectively!

I've studied this topic extensively, and have written and constructed thousands of e-mail messages to market insurance and investment products. Some have been complete duds. Others have hit home runs.

In this chapter, you're going to discover the optimal strategy for sending out e-mail messages to follow up and nurture and convert insurance and financial shoppers into policies and clients. You'll learn when to send them, how often, and when "too much" really IS too much.

You'll also get some e-mail templates you can swipe and deploy immediately. I usually share these templates only with my high-end Platinum-level clients, so you're in for a treat!

Let's Look at the Data

Researchers at Velocify did some interesting research. They studied the responses to hundreds of thousands of e-mail messages sent to consumers who were looking for insurance or financial services.

They analyzed the time of day the e-mail was received, the day of the week, and the timing in the overall sequence.

What they found was that the magic number of e-mail messages to send before dropping the prospect into a long-term campaign is five.

Said another way, imagine you have a prospect who inquires about a quote or an appointment. Perhaps he found you via your website or LinkedIn, or maybe he was a lead you bought from a lead provider.

After making five attempts to follow up with him via e-mail, if he doesn't reply, it is time to STOP e-mailing him with personal inquiries.

What you should DO instead is move him into a long-term, nurturing campaign. This could be a simple monthly newsletter that provides updates on your products, or a once-a-month "check in"-type e-mail to see if he's been helped. (I'll share an AMAZING e-mail later on that you can copy and use for this purpose. It has generated over $300,000 in premium so far).

Are You Among the 90 Percent Who Aren't Reaching Out *Enough*?

But here's the most surprising part of the study.

When insurance companies—big-time carriers—were put to the test, Velocify showed that only 6 percent of insurance buyers received anywhere near the optimal number of e-mail messages (four to six).

Only 5 percent were actually over-e-mailed (meaning they got more than five e-mail messages). And 89 percent—nine out of ten people—were either not e-mailed enough or not e-mailed at all. Shocking!

E-mail is one of the most affordable ways to reach a prospect. So why wouldn't you do everything you could to e-mail the prospect as much as possible?

A Winning E-mail Sequence

When I was growing what is today the largest health insurance lead generator in the country, we learned from our agents the importance of e-mailing a lead *immediately* after he requests a report. I'm talking, SECONDS.

Your content must be compelling, responsive, and help move the conversation along.

In order to help you with this, let me share with you a very powerful e-mail sequence that one of my clients is using. Before I share it, you'll notice that these e-mail messages are written a bit differently from what you're used to.

That's because they're NOT designed to sell insurance or an annuity. The *only* objective is to get a person on the phone or start a digital conversation via e-mail.

By the way, I do NOT recommend you use a simple e-mail platform such as Gmail or Outlook to do this for you. That would require too much tracking and manual work. Instead, consider using an autoresponder. These are widely available e-mail services where you write a set of e-mail messages in advance and they send it out for you.

GetResponse is a great one to start with, as is MailChimp. Both allow you to import leads into them so they can send out messages automatically.

OK, here are the templates!

E-mail #1: Goes out within one hour

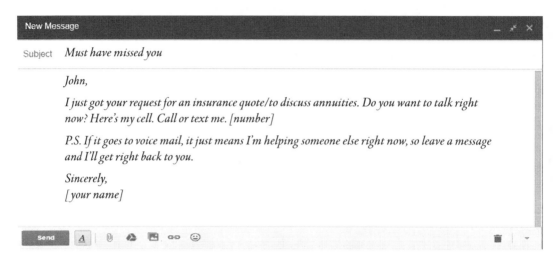

Notice that this message doesn't offer quotes. It doesn't try to sell the product. It just tries to be human and get to know the prospect.

Marketing Mastery Tip: A clever trick that works really well for getting high open rates is to use all lowercase letters in the subject line.

Look at the difference:

Option 1) must have missed you
Option 2) Must Have Missed You

Which of the two looks like it was written by a human and not a robot?
Exactly. Option 1.

E-mail #2: This e-mail can go out a day or two after the first one and is designed to follow up after someone has downloaded a report, for example, "The 15-Minute Retirement Readiness Plan" or "The Top 7 Secrets to Save on Your Insurance."

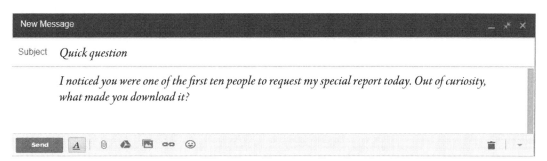

Now, there's a bit of a gray area here. Because this is an autoresponder, they could be the 110th person to request your report. The point is, pick a number that's plausible and works for you.

The goal is just to start a conversation.

We recently sent this to two hundred people who downloaded a report. Out of that two hundred, fifty replied with a very personal message. That's a 25 percent reply to an autoresponder!

And when people reply, read exactly what they tell you. This is their actual "problem solving gears" at work. It's almost like getting a 3-D view into their mind and seeing where they are in the decision-making process.

For example, when someone answers:

I downloaded it because I've been searching for how to make sense of annuities in my retirement plan and your report seemed to give some clarity to that.

. . . that's a GREAT insight!

Now, in your copywriting, or your conversation, or your next webinar, you can use that exact quote. For example:

Welcome to the call today. In today's meeting we're going to address how to make sense of annuities within your retirement plan.

By the way, the subject line "quick question" is one of my *highest*-converting subject lines of all time. It works for almost all situations because it looks like something you can quickly answer and then delete from your inbox.

Master Marketer Tip: *Use the responses you get — the exact words the person wrote — in your sales letter, presentation, webinar, or seminar. This will match the precise word patterns and language your prospects use when they're looking for your product or service.*

E-mail #3:

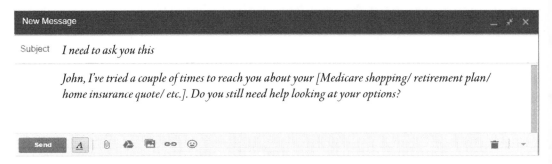

First off, that subject line is powerful.

We all have the impulse to answer questions when we're asked. So, if somebody says he needs to ask you something, it sounds pretty serious — and you listen.

The e-mail itself is also super simple. The only answer the prospect can give is yes or no. There's no complicated reply required, so he's more likely to answer.

E-mail #4:

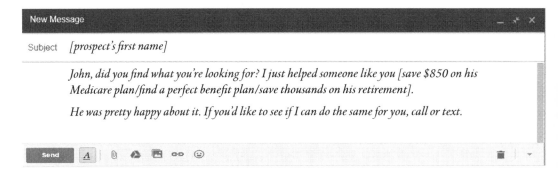

Again, this e-mail is simple and to the point.

It just asks the prospect if he has found what he was looking for and tells him that you just helped someone just like him. This stands out from other nurturing autoresponder e-mail messages because you're showing the person the value you can offer him.

In this case, it's saving money.

And the subject line is *amazing*. Just using the person's first name is one of the most powerful open-rate strategies you can use. And again, you can use it for any type of e-mail.

Just be careful not to use it too much, or your audience will catch on and stop replying.

E-mail #5:

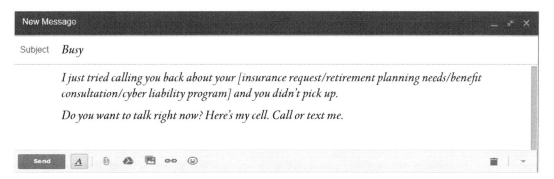

Subject: *Busy*

I just tried calling you back about your [insurance request/retirement planning needs/benefit consultation/cyber liability program] and you didn't pick up.

Do you want to talk right now? Here's my cell. Call or text me.

This one assumes that you've attempted to call the prospect at some point during this drip campaign. It's a really good one because most of the time, we really don't answer our phones. When somebody doesn't answer, we assume they're busy. So you're acknowledging that you understand the situation.

At this point, if the prospect has NOT replied, it's better to stop. Don't send any more e-mail messages, per Velocify's research.

As a bonus here, however, I'm going to give you a few more templates as well, so you have some alternatives. That way, you can pick and test WHICH of them work out well for you and decide whether five is your magic number or you do better by sending six or even seven e-mail messages.

E-mail #6:

This one is not for the faint of heart.

It's a bit of a hard close — but if you're that type of agent, it works exceedingly well. This is ideal if you use aged leads, work with thousands of leads a month, or process lots of orders each month — so it's mainly applicable to insurance.

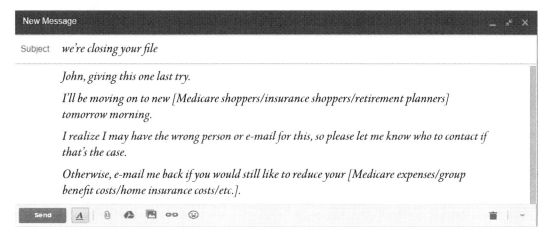

Subject: *we're closing your file*

John, giving this one last try.

I'll be moving on to new [Medicare shoppers/insurance shoppers/retirement planners] tomorrow morning.

I realize I may have the wrong person or e-mail for this, so please let me know who to contact if that's the case.

Otherwise, e-mail me back if you would still like to reduce your [Medicare expenses/group benefit costs/home insurance costs/etc.].

The subject line almost guarantees the e-mail will be opened.

Nobody likes to think they're being closed out, and this plays on the psychological need we all have to belong. As soon as somebody tells us we can't have something, we want it even more.

Then, the e-mail simply explains that you can help this person save money — but you have to move on.

Of course, you don't have to leave it on that note. You could send one more e-mail.

E-mail #7:

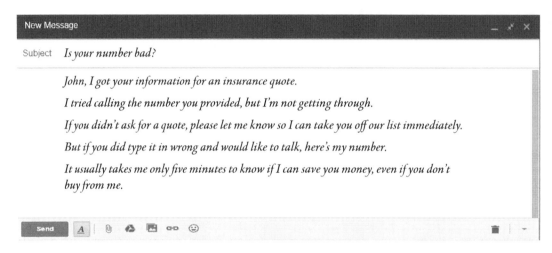

This is a friendlier way to finish off the nurturing sequence, and allows you to send seven e-mail messages before moving the prospect to the once-a-month newsletter cycle.

First, you tell him you tried to reach him. Then, you do him the courtesy of allowing him to get off your list — if that's really what he wants. (After all, we don't want to keep contacting people who don't want to be contacted. They're not our ideal prospects.)

Next, you restate your number, showing him you're easy to reach and letting him know it will be a short call, because it only takes you five minutes.

And here's the best part: "…even if you don't buy from me." That phrase shows that you're a very friendly advisor. You're not there to hard close him. You just want to give him some value — even if he proceeds to go and buy from another agent.

My Favorite Autoresponders

It's pretty easy to set something like this up. Most lead companies integrate with an autoresponder solution.

For health insurance agents, I suggest BrokerOffice by GoHealth. If you're in a different industry, you can integrate most of your lead capture forms on your site with a simple tool called GetResponse. There are many others, such as AWeber, Infusionsoft, and Office Autopilot, but I love the simplicity and the power of GetResponse, as well as their great customer service.

You can load all seven messages in about an hour. Then, set up a drip sequence triggered anytime somebody fills out a form to download a special report or watch a video on your website. And you'll quickly put yourself among the top 10 percent of agents who do e-mail marketing the right way.

Summary

In this chapter you discovered that the ideal number of e-mail messages to send out to a prospect before you drop them into a drip sequence is five. Any more e-mail messages, and you're risking looking desperate and losing them forever as a prospect.

You also got VIP access to some of my highest-converting e-mail templates that only my Platinum-level clients get (you're welcome!) to swipe and deploy on your follow-ups. Finally, we discussed the power of using autoresponders to automate your marketing and free up your time.

The Takeaway

☐ Review the autoresponder templates and choose five that work for you.

☐ Customize the content to your message and follow-up sequence.

☐ Subscribe to a tool like GetResponse or another autoresponder.

☐ Upload your messages and start using them in your follow-ups.

☐ Visit www.Theshiftnation.org to get access to these and more templates to test!

CHAPTER 26

How an Old-school, Direct-Response Marketing Strategy Can Unearth a Gold Mine of Prospects

"Big shots are only little shots who keep shooting."
—Christopher Morley

Application:
B2B,
B2C
Difficulty: Moderate
Time to implement: One to three hours
Cost to implement: $500 a month

There was a time when agent Gordon hated selling insurance. He was using the same old tactics as everybody else. But they weren't working.

He'd sit around, waiting for the phone to ring. He seemed to work nonstop but wasn't making much money. That's when he started to *SHIFT* the way he approached marketing.

SHIFT Your Focus and Your Position

Gordon said to himself, "I'm a business owner. And I want to work with people like me: people who eat, sleep, and drink their business."

So he started focusing on direct-response mailings. He wrote up simple yet highly specific postcards targeting small- to medium-sized business owners looking for a trusted advisor.

Not just somebody looking for the next cheapest policy.

To set himself apart from the competition, he started writing articles on topics that appealed to business owners. Every month, he'd send out these valuable mailers to his target market.

Over and over. Month after month.

And eventually, they'd ask for a quote.

Never Give Up

Gordon had especially good timing. The niche he was focusing on primarily used a national carrier that had cornered its market.

The carrier pulled out, and Gordon's mailings proved effective right from the get-go. (On average, though, people will take notice after five to seven mailings.)

Gordon mailed some business owners for four or five years before they finally called — fed up, but curious.

One contractor said, "You know, I was going to call you up and tell you to take me off your mailing list already. But then something happened with my agent and I finally thought, you know what, you've been mailing stuff to me for so long, I've got to give you a shot."

Gordon was able to save the contractor double digits!

And he'd turned a slightly annoyed lead into a hugely satisfied customer — who became a raving fan.

Most Agents Quit Too Soon—and That's a Mistake

The key to Gordon's strategy is to show up every month and to stay front and center in his prospect's mind. Most agents run campaigns for one or two months. They decide it doesn't work. So they stop.

But maybe if they'd sent just one more mailing, they could have closed a $20,000 or $30,000 account. They quit too soon.

Gordon's philosophy was simple: send mailings until they buy or die.

Never. Give. Up.

Position Yourself as a Trusted Partner

Another important aspect of Gordon's approach was showing the value he could provide. Remember, he was trying to set himself apart from the commoditization of the market. He wasn't just a person who could help the client get the cheapest policy; he was a trusted advisor to people *just like him:* hardworking business owners facing daily challenges and trying to overcome them.

Gordon's goal was to craft messages that showed he was an expert in his market's field. That he could be a one-stop shop. And a partner.

Effective Copywriting Strategies

Gordon accomplished this through very effective copywriting strategies that he learned from one of the masters of the art of copywriting.

He had become so dissatisfied with his business that he was ready to throw in the towel.

But instead of giving up, he doubled down. He committed to waking up an hour earlier and staying up an hour later to hone his craft.

Over the course of fifty-two weeks, he found a lot of extra time. And he used that time to teach himself the art of direct-response copywriting.

The Gold Mine Is Within Your Very Own Book of Business

So how can you build your own direct-response marketing strategy? First, look within your own book of business. Print out a list of your commercial clients.

Most people don't realize that they have lots of unmined niches within their own book.

Start listing those niches:

- Auto-repair shops
- Used-car dealerships
- Contractors
- Restaurants
- Pizza shops

While you're doing it, check out the numbers. You'll inevitably find a niche or two where you've already found success.

Then, develop marketing materials that address that niche. Start mailing them out.

And don't stop until you've got a client.

The Takeaway 👍

☐ Examine your book of business for niches you already serve.

☐ Develop marketing materials that target those niches. Focus on value. Study the masters of direct-response copywriting for maximum effect.

☐ Keep sending mailers and don't stop — remember — until they buy or die.

☐ Devote a regular block of time every day to mastering a skill that will move you closer to your goal.

☐ If you're generating your own leads, follow the strategies and guidelines above for success.

☐ No matter your lead-generation method, follow up quickly and consistently.

CHAPTER 27

How One Agent Wrote $1.5 Million in Premium by Teaching Free Social Media Classes

"The best marketing doesn't feel like marketing."
—Tom Fishburne

Application:
B2B
Difficulty: Moderate
Time to implement: Three to five hours a month
Cost to implement: $200+

If you like to help people, you'll like this next story and the powerful lessons it shares. And if you've been looking for a way to make a difference in your community, you'll LOVE it.

You're going to read about an agency that has at its helm someone with deep personal beliefs, who loves to give back. You'll discover how he built one of the fastest-growing agencies in his city that is quickly chipping away market share from the "old agency down the block." His strategy is simple but profoundly effective: education.

Meet Chris

Chris Paradiso was introduced to me by a friend who works with ACORD (Association for Cooperative Operations Research and Development). From the moment I got on the phone with him, I could tell he was a guy who was passionate about what he believed in. So much so that one can't help but feel inspired by him.

He runs a personal- and commercial-lines agency out of Stafford Springs, Connecticut. From the outset, he placed a big emphasis on giving back and education, but not just *insurance* education; he wanted to help his local business community grow and elevate.

Chris is particularly passionate about social media and the power it gives us to reach out to people and share ideas. Again, not just ideas about insurance.

Chris's Facebook page is a great example of how three-dimensional an agency can be. It includes pictures of his family, employees, and customers; of him supporting and hosting local events; of him supporting other businesses; you name it.

With almost four thousand likes, Paradiso's agency Facebook page mixes insurance tips with a heavy focus on local community outreach. https://www.facebook.com/InsuranceCT

As his agency grew, Chris saw the value in hiring a full-time social media expert to help build his community and empower it. That's how much he believes in the power of online social networks.

He's an especially big fan of YouTube. His agency actually interviews satisfied clients and uploads those videos to their channel to share with everyone.

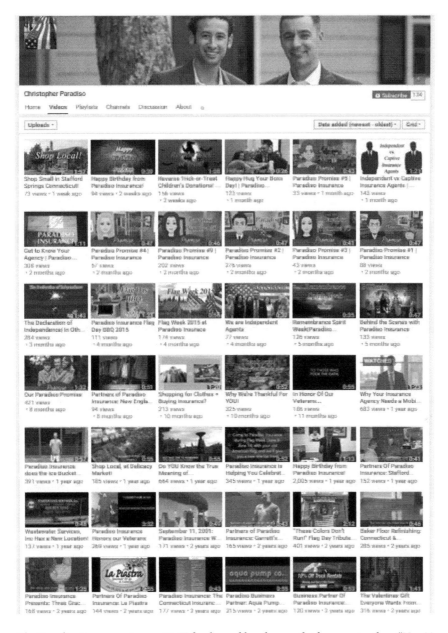

The Paradiso Insurance Agency YouTube channel has dozens of videos ranging from "Hug Your Boss Day" to "Why Your Agency Needs a Mobile App" to insurance tips and client testimonials. https://www.youtube.com/user/paradisoinsurance/videos.

But Chris doesn't stop there; he goes one step further.

He holds classes in his local business community to teach fellow business owners how to use social media and brand themselves. The classes are not just for his clients; they're for everybody (including competitors).

Why Chris Gives Away His "Competitive Advantage"—and Why You Should, Too

Chris's position is this: "We want to help our fellow business-owners succeed so we're going to teach you how to use Facebook."

While Chris hosts the class, he has a consultant actually run it. In the process, Chris learns a lot about his prospective customers and builds relationships.

What's clever is that Chris knows that many of those who attend aren't interested in doing business with him. They already have an advisor, and he respects that. He doesn't want the people taking his class to break their current relationship. He just wants them to build a new relationship with him.

And in the end, this strategy benefits him. Here's an example of how it works.

How a Four-Year-Old Lead Turned into a Loyal Client

Chris recently received a Facebook message from a woman who took one of his social media classes — four years ago!

She wasn't interested in switching agents at the time. She'd spent half a day learning about Facebook and went on her way. But then, out of the blue, her agent canceled her homeowners insurance — an agent she had been with for TWENTY YEARS!

She'd called the agent to follow up and make sure the policy was renewed. He'd kept saying there was plenty of time, and not to worry.

Well, he forgot!

Her family's insurance was about to lapse. The agent said he was so sorry and that he would call her back within twenty-four hours.

Twenty-four hours later, she still hadn't heard from him.

The woman remembered Chris from his class. She found him on Facebook and told him she wanted to meet with him to discuss her insurance. She hadn't been ready to make a change four years earlier — but she was now.

Her agent had messed up. But Chris had made such a great impression with his classes that he was the first person to come to mind when she thought about dumping her agent.

Chris got back to her the next day. He wrote two new pieces of business . . . from an interaction that had happened <u>nearly half-a-decade earlier</u>.

In all, Chris has written at least $1.5 million worth of business by focusing on relationships using this seminar strategy.

You can easily replicate this technique in your community. Perhaps you have a certain business skill that would be valuable to share. You can teach hiring practices. Account techniques. Networking principles. Or grab a chapter from Chris and collaborate with a local expert on a hot topic that people would love to know about, such as marketing, lead generation, or sales. (A quick search on LinkedIn in your city will net you a ton of results to choose from.)

You can find low-cost, professional spaces in which to hold your classes and meetings using Liquidspace.com. A really good-looking conference room can cost as little as $15 per hour.

www.liquidpace.com is a free service that allows you to browse office space, meeting rooms, and coworking locations for your meetings and events.

One of my Platinum-level clients is taking the LinkedIn strategies I've taught him and using that as a basis for teaching local businesses via seminars and webinars.

Remember that being seen as a leader in your community isn't about you; it's about others. It's about connecting, adding value, and staying available.

Summary

What you just read about is a strategy that will take you about six months to get off the ground, but that could be worth $1.5 million in premium — as it was to Chris, because he stuck with it. Using a simple topic such as "Small-Business Marketing Basics" or "Hiring Best Practices: How to Hire Rock Stars Who Will Soar Your Sales," you can start small. If you don't like to present, find someone who does. You do the introduction and conclusion. Your partner gets a free audience, and you get to draw a crowd. It's a win-win!

You can find thousands of local experts who might be available to you through a simple search on LinkedIn.

You can use your current facilities for training to start out or find a hotel, or you can use the LiquidSpace app on your smart phone to find a local place to use. Then use Meetup.com to share your event with other people in the area — for free.

The Takeaway 👍

☐ Offer free community classes and teach a strategy or technique to business owners.

☐ Don't over-pitch during the event. Let this be about your offering education.

☐ Stick with it for six months, scheduling one event every one to two months.

☐ Over time, stay in touch. Build a relationship. It may end up turning into new business in ways you'd never expected.

CHAPTER 28

How to Generate $37,000 Worth of FREE Traffic in under Six Months with This No-Cost YouTube Hack

"Whether you think you can or think you can't, you're right."
—Henry Ford

Application: B2B, B2C
Difficulty: Easy
Time to implement: Two hours
Cost to implement: Free

If you were to meet Randy in person, you'd fall in love with the guy. He's humble, caring, and really just wants to help people. He's also very shy — which you'd think would be a problem for an agent who wants to get on YouTube.

But in this chapter, you're going to learn about a very ninja technique I taught him that got him close to $40,000 in free traffic on YouTube. He got there by doing just a few little tweaks to his video, which took him five minutes.

I'll teach you how to use the same technique yourself, and what to say in your video so that you come across naturally and feel more comfortable in front of the camera.

By the way, if you're at ALL uncomfortable in front of the camera, I know how you feel.

Five or six years ago, I did my very first YouTube video.

The lighting was terrible. There was a huge glare on the whiteboard behind me. I had no fancy video equipment or anything like that.

I was so nervous that this five-minute video took me SIXTEEN takes to get right.

Somebody even outed me in the comments: "Good video. You need a MICROPHONE, though!"

But even this cheesy video made me over $100,000!

I did it all with a three-step formula and a simple, five-minute optimization hack.

Meet Randy and His First Video

Pros and Cons of the Affordable Care Act, Obamacare

This is a screenshot of Randy Pfeiffer's YouTube video. Now, Randy is not a big-time agent. He has a small office in Grand Junction, Colorado, and he'd never done a YouTube video before.

So I showed him exactly what I'm going to show you now.

The theme of his first video was the pros and cons of the Affordable Care Act.

You'll notice that it's just him. No fancy lighting. No Tom Ford suit. Just his friendly face, coming to you from his office, with a photograph in the background. That's it.

But here's what this "little video that could" did for Randy.

- Within six months, he had 8,547 views.
- Within a year, he had 18,617 views.

And he didn't pay for a single visitor!

"How did he do that?" you may be asking.

Read on, my friend. It's surprisingly easier than you think.

How Much Your Free YouTube Video Is Worth

To appreciate what quality visitors mean in dollar and cents, you have to keep in mind that there's another way that Randy could have done this.

Option One: The Expensive Option

He could have bid on the keyword phrase "Obamacare in Colorado," where he happens to live. This would have cost him $1.95 per click. Multiply that by the number of YouTube views, and it would have cost him $40,000.

Option Two: The Cheating-for-No-Good-Reason Option

He could have gone over to fiverr.com and hired a service to deliver one thousand views to his video for five bucks. Sounds like cheating your way to the top, and some people do use this technique. But . . . are you interested in views or LEADS?

Many of these services get robot views from locations such as China, India, Kazakhstan, and other locations where you don't sell insurance. In other words, they are useless.

Option Three: The Quality-Traffic Option

Use solid ranking strategies and embed these into your video in order to attract the kind of viewers that can actually do business with you.

The Three-Step Formula for Recording Your First Video

First, we have to determine what you're going to say in your video. This question alone is the reason why most advisors never start; they don't know how to structure their talk!

I've honed a very simple formula that originated in the military that works in any market and any niche. It just requires a little *SHIFT* in the way you think about videos.

Here's the no-fail formula for creating your first set of educational videos.

Step One: Tell them what you're going to tell them.
Step Two: Tell them.
Step Three: Tell them what you told them.

If you've been paying careful attention, you know that I've been using the same formula throughout this book, to help you absorb the information more easily.

Here's how to use the formula in a video:

Step One: "In this video, you're going to learn . . ."
Step Two: "Here's what this is . . ." (You explain what you're talking about.)
Step Three: "This is what you've learned in this video . . ."

Here's an example.

> *Hi. My name is Jeremiah Desmarais, and in this video, you're going to learn how to save money on insurance by using a simple three-step formula.*
>
> *Here's what the formula is: you need to . . . And that's the formula.*
>
> *In this video, you've learned a simple three-step formula. You see how easy that was? Now it's your turn. If you haven't recorded a simple video yet, I challenge you to do that right now. Yes, right NOW! Chances are, you have a smartphone nearby, or a tablet, and can do a practice session right now.*
>
> *Don't worry about doing it correctly or very professionally; just DO it! You'll see how simple it is and can then start moving forward on your path to digital mastery.*
>
> *I'm rooting for you!*

Bonus YouTube Tricks

Once you've completed your video, here are a few mastery-level tips for making an effective video:

- Keep your video between three and five minutes long so that you don't risk boring people.
- Grab them in the beginning with a really good hook: "I'm going to share the weird trick most people don't know that can lower your insurance by hundreds."
- Use words such as "steps," "formulas," and "systems." This kind of terminology tells viewers that you've thought your information through and you're not just winging it. Example: "I'm going to show you my Three-Step Retirement-Maximization System to make sure you get the most Social Security benefits when you retire."

Get Your Video on the Front Page of Google

A few years ago, I was invited by an FMO/GA to give a talk about digital marketing to a small group of two hundred or so advisors. To help promote the event, I recorded a short, one-minute video and uploaded it to YouTube.

Using a few of the ranking strategies I'm about to show you, I got that video ranked on the FIRST page of Google in fewer than twenty-four hours!

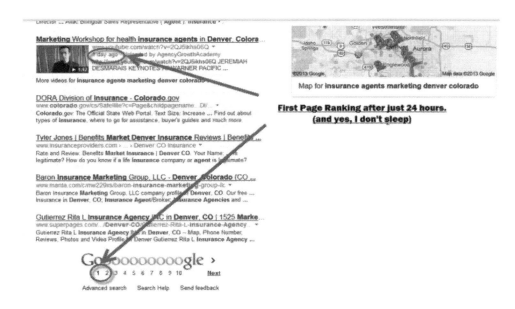

Map for insurance agents marketing denver colorado

**First Page Ranking after just 24 hours.
(and yes, I don't sleep)**

In just eighteen hours, it was ranked on the first page.

There's a very important reason for this:

Google *loves* YouTube videos!

If you optimize your video the right way, Google will rank a video above a blog post or a press release.

How to Rank Your First Video so Google Will LOVE It

When you upload your video, here's what you'll see on YouTube's back end:

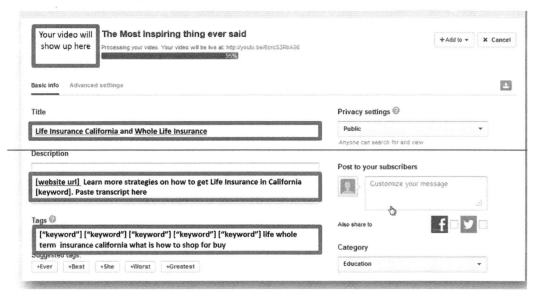

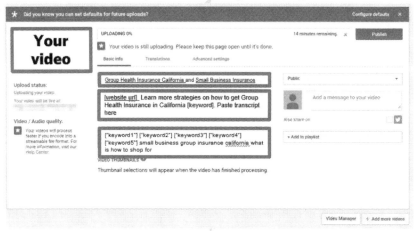

In the top left-hand corner, you'll see the icon for your video, and underneath, there are three areas to optimize:

1. The title
2. The description
3. The tags

Optimize Your Title

In the title area, include your primary and secondary keywords as frequently as possible.

For example, if I'm selling life insurance in California, I'll be sure to include the phrases "Life Insurance California" — which is a primary keyword — and "Whole Life Insurance," a secondary keyword.

Here's a space to write down some of your ideas for keywords:

Keyword idea: _____

Keyword idea: _____

Keyword idea: _____

Keyword idea: _____

Keyword idea: _____

Optimize Your Description

This next part is really important.

In the description, *put your website address first.*

You don't really want people to stay on your video. You want them to click through to your site, where they become leads.

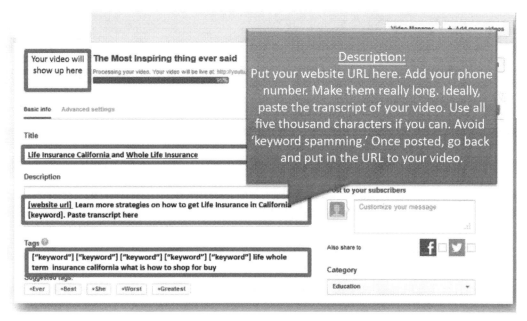

And here's a mastery-level tip:

You can even combine this strategy with an auto-dialer account. As traffic comes to your site from your videos, people will enter their contact information — or at least you hope they will. You can integrate most web forms with an auto-dialer program so that all incoming leads will be called right away.

Be sure to try to use all 5,000 characters allowed in the description. This is very important because Google looks at this content to see if it's relevant to your audience. If it is, it will rank the video higher.

For example, if you're recording a video about life insurance, you'll say that term many times throughout your script. Doing the same in the description tells Google, "Optimize this for 'life insurance.'"

A simple hack for getting this done is to get your video transcribed. You can hire a transcriber for about $5 per minute of video from fiverr.com. Once you get the transcription back, edit it for accuracy and copy it to your description area.

Optimize Your Tags

Finally, there are your tags.

This is where you tell Google the specific keywords you want to rank for. Enter all your relevant keywords without quotation marks.

Here, the relevant keywords would be:

- Life
- Whole
- Term
- Insurance
- California

Now, here's a really cool trick! In addition to the regular keywords, there are a few keywords that are "buying signals." These are words that people use when they're typing something into Google that they seriously want to buy or learn about.

Here are a few:

- What is
- How to
- Shop for
- Buy

People use these magic words most often when they're ready to buy: "SHOP FOR California term insurance," for example.

Be sure to put quotation marks around the words you *really* want to rank for — but don't repeat them more than once.

Now, Drive Traffic

Once you've recorded your video, you want to drive traffic to it — because, if no one sees it, it's useless.

So grab the link to your YouTube video and do the following:

1. Post it on your blog.
2. Post it on LinkedIn forums in a very classy way, e.g., "Hey, I just recorded this new video that dispels a lot of the myths that people have about [blank]. I thought you'd enjoy it."
3. Post it on your Facebook page.
4. Post it in the comments section of any relevant news sites. For example, there are articles published every day about annuities, retirement, insurance, and investing online. Many have sections at the bottom where you can comment on the article. These are FREE ways to post your YouTube link. Just thank the author for the article and say you've created a video that helps build on what he just wrote.

Now, your nifty video can be seen far and wide.

Summary

OK, so that was a bit technical, but I know you can handle it. After all, you bought this book because you wanted actionable strategies to generate more leads, right? Not just a collection of platitudes and vague suggestions that have been rehashed time and again! So I'm bringing the goods and hoping you'll get tremendous value from it.

You just got my top-secret YouTube ranking strategy and how to record your first video. We reviewed how to break down your video and what to say, step by specific step. Then, we dove into some advanced tips to get free traffic to it.

Now, all that's left is for you to record your video!

The Takeaway

- ☐ Record your video using the three-step formula.
- ☐ Post it on YouTube and use the tips above to optimize the title, description, and tags for great Google rankings.
- ☐ Post a link to the video on your blog, in LinkedIn forums, on your Facebook page, and in the comments of online news articles.

CHAPTER 29

How to Create Million-Dollar Production Webinars

*"If you're looking for the next big thing, and you're looking where
everyone else is, you're looking in the wrong place."*
—Mark Cuban

Application: B2B,
B2C
Difficulty: Advanced
Time to implement: One week
Cost to implement: $1,000

Jeff was the founder of an FMO that had an incredible story and track of success with its first base of agents. Before I met him, he was recruiting advisors through his regular speaking engagements at various industry conferences. He was a passionate and dynamic speaker who had an important message to share, and advisors were naturally attracted to him.

But, despite his charisma and charm, Jeff had difficulty ramping up his firm's recruitment efforts. After all, there are only so many events at which to speak – and spending time away from one's family can be wearisome.

I introduced him to one of my recruitment techniques that could effectively translate his passion and charisma into a twenty-four-hour presentation designed to sift, select, and recruit advisors without any effort on his part; it's completely automatic.

My question to him was, "How would you like to have your best sales presentation running on autopilot, twenty-four hours a day, seven days a week, without your even being there?"

I'm sure you know his answer.

"Well, you can," I said, "with on-demand webinars."

These provide what feels like a live experience — but the entire thing is prerecorded.

I've used webinars to help to build one of the fastest-growing companies in insurance services — currently #17 on the Inc. 5,000 list. It's the same tool that I've used to train hundreds of thousands of agents in more than fifty-one countries around the world.

In this chapter, you're going to learn how I helped Jeff's FMO become one of the fastest growing in the country, exploding at a rate of 611 percent growth in just sixty days. We held a series of recruiting webinars — all on autopilot — and every day, new agents would sign up.

Shockingly, this is one of the least utilized tools among financial advisors and insurance agents today. Let's you and I fix that!

The Different Types of Webinars

First, you have to understand that the two basic webinar delivery methods:

1. **Live:** These account for 99 percent of all webinars in the insurance and financial space.
2. **On demand:** These are rarely used but infinitely powerful. They offer almost all of the elements of a live webinar, except you don't have to be there.

Live webinars are amazing because you can feed off the energy of the crowd and employ call-and-response techniques, real-time polling, and live webcams. The interaction stirs up excitement and enthusiasm for your program.

You can do the same with on-demand webinars — without even showing up.

How Automated Webinars Generate Leads 24/7

As I said, this multimillion-dollar webinar strategy is virtually untapped by insurance and financial professionals. My clients and I have used them to generate hundreds of thousands of dollars in profits in just the insurance and financial space alone.

Imagine taking the BEST presentation you've ever given on a webinar, recording it, then broadcasting it at specific times that work best for your prospects. That's the strategy in a nutshell.

A prospect signs up virtually on a simple landing page, chooses a date and time that works for him, and e-mail robots follow up to make sure he shows up on time.

Sample on-demand webinar sign-up page I've used in one of my funnels.

Perhaps you are wondering, what about engagement? Not a problem. You can use Skype to chat with people while they're signed on to the on-demand webinar! Just set a reminder to be available and have Skype open at the appropriate time, so you can quickly reply to attendees.

Are you getting the picture? Instead of having to commit your time to offering a webinar every single week, you can simply record one and broadcast it, week after week, month after month.

Here's a wireframe of a very high-converting, on-demand webinar we built for one GA. It's full of my best nurturing strategies.

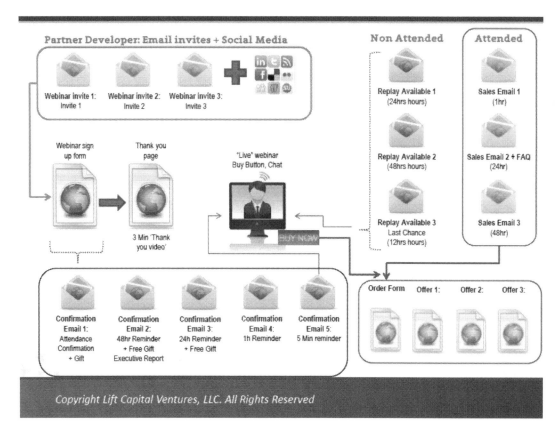

What to Broadcast

There are several topics that are particularly well suited to on-demand webinars.

1. Recruiting for general agencies or FMOs (a.k.a. "opportunity webinars")
2. Group benefits information updates (perfect for ACA changes)
3. Investment overviews for retirement advisors (great for evenings)
4. Special-guest interviews with industry notables (any market)
5. Risk management, cyber liability, and other topics of interest to commercial-lines prospects
6. New skills for local business owners (with your firm as the sponsoring party)

How to Generate Great Attendance

You can grow your attendee list using a simple opt-in form on your website. You can also buy traffic and send it to that page via LinkedIn or Facebook.

Include a call to action, such as: *Join this executive briefing on how to prepare yourself for retirement/how to prepare yourself for the Affordable Care Act/how four Chicago CFOs handle business/insurance challenges.*

This is a great alternative to writing a white paper, by the way. Invite your core audience — CFOs or HR managers — to a presentation where you'll discuss the challenges they face.

If those people are too hard to reach, you can build partnerships with attorneys, CPAs, TPAs, legal experts, HR consultants — anybody and everybody who could serve as a referral — and invite them to share it with their list.

Even better, invite a local CPA to be interviewed. Have him invite his list too. This makes the CPA seem like more of an authority in the eyes of his market, and helps you get more leads in the process.

Offer an Added Bonus in Return for a Testimonial or Review

Repurposing your content is a great way to get more mileage out of everything you do.

For example, take your best webinar and turn it into a white paper you can use to generate even more leads for your office. This can be done easily by hiring a transcriber from fiverr.com — the online market I mentioned earlier — to transcribe the audio. You'll pay maybe $10 for every five minutes. So for around $100, you can have your entire webinar on paper. Then, if you don't want to do it yourself, hire an editor on Elance who can turn it into a polished white paper for about $10 a page.

Now, you have an on-demand webinar generating leads twenty-four hours a day — *and* a complimentary white paper to offer qualified participants! And how do they qualify? Read on.

Encourage Your Audience to Leave You Feedback to Get a Bonus

Would you like to collect great testimonials every week that you can use in your future marketing? Great! Then let me teach you a really stealthy strategy for generating hundreds of recommendations in a short period of time.

At the end of your webinar, simply ask your guests to e-mail you a favorable review of the webinar or include it in a LinkedIn recommendation. Promise them that if they do so, you'll send them not only the slides and recording of the talk (because everybody will ask for these), but also, the entire transcript. I have seen people generate more than one hundred reviews on LinkedIn, all positive, with this strategy. If you're going to provide value, you should treat it as valuable. Don't just give your material away for free; make participants do a little extra work for it.

Let's be honest. If you're just putting generalities out into the market (which I'm sure you'd never do), then you don't deserve the recommendations of your listeners. That should be all the motivation you need to deliver consistently outstanding, game-changing content with every event you create.

As a result, you'll have CFOs, HR managers, attorneys—really, anyone you designate as your target market—writing accolades on your LinkedIn profile. Then you can use my outbound LinkedIn marketing strategies to boost your credibility and broaden your reach.

Start Recording and Broadcasting Webinars *Today*

Of all the automated webinar platforms I've tested, StealthSeminar has the best support—so I recommend it for help in building your webinar. For a couple hundred bucks, they'll set up the entire presentation for you and make sure it works well. They'll even build a series of e-mail messages so that if people sign up but don't attend, they're encouraged to attend the next one.

After people register, they'll receive confirmation e-mail messages and reminders to ensure they show up. And Stealth Seminar will broadcast your program whenever you tell it to! You can even set it up so that at the very end of the webinar, you can switch to LIVE mode and do a real-time, fifteen-minute question-and-answer session.

Summary

I've just shared an incredible webinar strategy that I was paid over $100,000 to develop. You saw the precise sequence I used to build it, the psychology behind it, and the tools I used to make it happen.

You learned about the power of on-demand webinars and how they can save hours of your busy schedule by running on autopilot, on-demand, twenty-four hours a day, seven days a week—sifting, qualifying, and closing people for you while you're off doing the things you love.

Deep down, you know that the knowledge you've accumulated over the years is worth charging for. My hope is that you will use the skills and tactics I've provided you with to take the first leap toward asking for it!

The Takeaway

- ☐ Use a platform such as StealthSeminar to record, schedule, and automate your webinar.

- ☐ Invite influencers and decision-makers in your target market, or professionals who could be a strong source of referrals.

- ☐ Offer your webinar on demand.

- ☐ Have the webinar transcribed and turned into a white paper.

- ☐ Offer the white paper to attendees who leave a positive recommendation on LinkedIn.

CHAPTER 30

The Seven-Figure Client-Qualification Webinar Strategy

"The more you can dream, the more you can do."
—Michael Korda

Application:
B2B,
B2C
Difficulty: Moderate
Time to implement: One week of planning
Cost to implement: Free

At this point, dear future marketing maven, you may be wondering whether webinars can work with high-net-worth clients or people who own large organizations. I mean, this can only work with smaller insurance- or retirement-plan shoppers, right?

To answer that question, let me share a fascinating case study of a tax consultancy with affluent clients that built a multimillion-dollar practice with webinars. They used a unique "pay-to-play" model that made every lead pay for itself — even if they never bought a single product.

While you go through this model, I want to invite you to consider whether this methodology could help you start charging UP FRONT for your products and services.

Turning a Free Consultation into a Small Webinar Fee

The process is simple and straightforward.

The advisory firm ran radio ads in its target area, offering a free consultation with IRS-trained attorneys on how people earning $400,000+ can ethically reduce their taxes and save for the future.

When someone called in, he was qualified, and if he was a good fit for the program, the sales rep invited him to attend a webinar for $199.

Yes, the firm CHARGED to take the next step!

Charging a fee for its small group webinars helped weed out the tire-kickers who would never buy. It also served to assign a high level of value to the information that would be shared.

Could you start charging even a small fee for initial consultations? How might that affect the quality of clients with whom you work?

The firm I've described also offered a 100 percent money-back guarantee to any attendee who didn't save money at tax time by using its strategies. And, toward the end of the webinar, they offered participants an in-depth, one-on-one consultation with one of their IRS attorneys for just $1,000. Anyone who opted for that could deduct the $199 cost of the webinar from the $1,000.

This brilliant strategy is called "ascension." It constantly moves someone up the buying category by tapping into his commitment at each stage in the process.

The same process can be used offline for retirement or Social Security seminars. An advisor first offers a two-to-three-hour seminar, followed by an in-person meeting of similar duration, and finally, a follow-up presentation. (In this case, participants are investing time in the process, not money.)

The Psychology of Staggered Commitments

The strategy used by the advisory firm worked because of something called "staggered commitments." As participants completed the first part of the sales process, they became committed and engaged. It was easy to get them to open their wallets a bit.

Then, in the second step of the process, they were asked to open their wallets a little wider — this time, to the tune of $1,000. So, they began a relationship with the firm for a small cost and then moved through a series of stages that delivered more and more value and had bigger and bigger price tags.

By the way, another brilliant piece of this strategy involved the prospect sending his tax returns from the previous two years to the firm in advance, for upfront analysis. This led to an even greater commitment on the part of the prospect. Once he'd put in the time it took to find and send his old returns, he was on his way to a full investment in the process.

A major investment on the part of the client started with just a few hundred dollars.

Brilliant.

Closing the Sale with a Final Commitment

Back to the consultation with the IRS attorney.

At the end of the $1,000 consultation, the prospect is fully engaged. The agency has a complete picture of his financial situation and is fairly certain it can save him at least $10,000 to $20,000 in taxes the next time he files.

At this point, the agency makes him an offer: let us work with you [for anywhere from $10,000 on up], and we guarantee we'll save you at least double that.

This model has generated millions of dollars in sales for the tax-consulting business, which has become one of the fastest-growing companies in its market.

Your Knowledge Is Worth the Price of Admission

Now, you may not think you can charge that much for your knowledge, but that's a limiting mind-set. You absolutely can!

Right now, people are buying books, courses, and seminars offering information you're giving away for free in an attempt to get clients! Clients just like yours are paying experts — who don't earn a commission or an override — for valuable advice on structuring benefits.

One very smart St. Louis consulting firm specializing in management consulting built an entirely new business vertical charging companies $5,000 to analyze how the Affordable Care Act would affect them. Once the firm delivered its analysis, it offered other options, from which it profited handsomely.

An enterprising writer wrote a book on how to use life insurance as a personal "bank" and it became a *New York Times* bestseller, launching a newsletter and a national radio show. While the writer doesn't sell a single policy, he partnered with an FMO to create a lead program for advisors. The writer sells the leads that come in through the book and radio show to advisors and earns an override on their production that is managed through the FMO.

There are many divergent ways to leverage expertise. What I'm trying to get you to appreciate is that your knowledge has incredible value, and people will be willing to pay top dollar for it!

Work with a Consultant and Share the Wealth

Perhaps you're thinking, *But, by law, I'm not* ethically *allowed to charge for this stuff.*

Not a problem.

Bring your concept to a management consultant who has some experience in insurance but who can't write a policy. Teach him the idea (the easiest way would be to send him a copy of this book with a note). Then put an agreement in place and execute it.

Now, you can charge the consultant a marketing fee for putting it together. You're not the one giving the advice — but once the consultant fully qualifies a prospect, guess who he will refer him to? You!

And if you're allowed to pay for referrals, you can reward the consultant. Now, you have a game-changing strategy. The marketing cost is already covered because people are paying to consult with you, your entity, or your partner.

Summary

You've just jumped down the rabbit hole into one of the most profitable strategies you can implement in the sales process: getting paid up front for your advice. This creates a self-liquidating lead that pays for itself and results in zero-cost insurance or financial-services leads, or even a new profit center for your practice.

By using staggered commitments, you can prequalify prospects and move them up a value chain of service offerings that help you get paid in advance and avoid dealing with any but the most motivated and committed prospects.

What could you start charging for your advice today? Who, in your community, is actively looking for your services and willing to pay for them? How could you serve those people at a higher level by itemizing the benefits of doing business with you and attaching a price tag to it?

The Takeaway

- ☐ Run ads in your market offering a free thirty-minute consultation on an issue affecting your target market.

- ☐ Invite those you consult with to a webinar with a small price tag attached.

- ☐ At the end of the webinar, invite them to a more in-depth consultation for a higher fee.

- ☐ Then, close the sale by obtaining the final commitment.

- ☐ Not allowed to charge for webinars or seminars? Work with a consultant who can implement your plan and refer clients back to you. Post a message on LinkedIn forums where these consultants spend time, to attract the right one.

CHAPTER 31

How to Launch 3-D Direct-Mail Pieces That Command Attention

"Fortune favors the bold."
—Virgil

Application: B2B,
B2C
Difficulty: Easy
Time to implement: One week
Cost to implement: $2 to $5 per unit

How many e-mail messages do you get each day?

You probably don't count them anymore, but a recent study by the Radicati Group[1] found that the average businessperson gets an average of eighty-four e-mail messages a day — seventy-one of which are legitimate. If you break that down into work hours, that's almost nine e-mail messages per hour that require a response. Yipes! No wonder we are becoming more and more unfocused and distracted!

Think about how your prospect's inbox might look right now. Overstuffed and chock-full of messages, no doubt.

It's no wonder that smart advisors and agents are turning to the LEAST-crowded inbox today: the mailbox.

---

1   http://www.radicati.com/wp/wp-content/uploads/2011/05/Email-Statistics-Report-2011-2015-Executive-Summary.pdf

Margaret's Move from the Inbox to the Mailbox

Margaret is a savvy commercial-lines advisor who has been using e-mail marketing techniques and LinkedIn to drive meetings with qualified decision-makers in Kansas City companies to discuss workers' comp, cyber liability, and group benefits.

After spending years honing her craft, she decided to try out a new method of marketing to supplement her already-successful digital strategies: direct mail.

Before you groan and say, "That doesn't work anymore," consider this: according to the Direct Marketing Association's 2015 annual study, direct mail outperforms all digital channels *combined* by nearly 600 percent.

That's SIX HUNDRED PERCENT! That means, for the same investment you'd put into e-mail or display ads online, you'd get six times the result!

The big guys use direct mail all the time — American Express, Chase Bank, Comcast — multibillion-dollar companies. Because they know it works.

Meet the Next Step in the Evolution of Direct Mail: 3-D Mail

Instead of dedicating this chapter to simple form-letter or postcard strategies, I want to invite you to make a *SHIFT* in your marketing mix by learning about a more fringe area of the direct-response industry that very few advisors are using profitably: the 3-D direct-mail market.

These unique direct-mail pieces are called "3-D" because their pieces are literally three-dimensional. You may have heard it called "lumpy" mail.

It could be a pill bottle because "You've got a headache we're going to solve"; a physical boomerang to get people to "come back to us"; a vinyl bank bag with a zippered top that arrives with your name on it.

It's like nothing you've ever seen.

Creating Your Own "Wow" Factor

In the process of writing this chapter, I interviewed Travis Lee, an internationally known expert in the direct-response field. He's the co-founder and president of 3D Mail Results and is the behind-the-scenes resource for some of the biggest direct-response names in the industry. And he generates massive returns for thousands of businesses each year through innovative marketing strategies.

BOOK BONUS: There's an in-depth hour-long interview I conducted with Travis in the Bonus section. Just go to www.Theshiftnation.org to download and listen to it. It's full of great tips and ideas for insurance and financial practices!

His unique, tested, and proven marketing methodology has generated millions in sales for hundreds of businesses, from sole proprietorships run around the kitchen table to national and international businesses selling millions of pieces a year.

He's consistently shown positive returns of 200 to 3,500 percent.

Sample elements from a threeGiveaways from a self-mailer campaign that revolves around making and/or saving money.

You can imagine how surprised and intrigued a prospect will be when he receives one of these in the mail.

"The 'wow' factor is multiplied, versus just regular mail," Travis says.

The Psychology behind "Lumpy Mail"

"It's all about pattern interruption," he says.

People aren't used to receiving something like this in the mail. Imagine living in New York City and seeing a cowboy riding a horse down the street. You'd stop and look, right?

Studies have shown that you have about 3.5 seconds to grab a prospect's attention. That's in any medium: websites, e-mail messages, billboards, Yellow Pages ads, direct mail, rack cards, you name it.

But, if you can interrupt the pattern and grab their attention for a few seconds longer, your marketing will be that much more effective.

Here's another way to look at it: The average American is exposed to thirty-five hundred to thirty-eight hundred marketing messages every single day. We're so used to them that we hardly even see them.

These innovative direct-mail pieces break through.

Margaret's Breakthrough 3-D Marketing Strategy

In an effort to get more C-level appointments onto her calendar, Margaret and I implemented a systematic three-touch program using 3-D mail — specifically, the money approach.

In the first mailer, the CEO gets a vinyl bank bag on his desk with a well-written letter inside, with a core message something like this:

I've sent you this bank bag because I believe that after spending fifteen minutes with me on the phone, you'll know how to fill your deposits with more cash. You can do this by using my seven-step method to minimize workers' comp claims and negotiate your current insurance rates with carriers — something most insurance agents don't even know is possible and would never attempt.

The vinyl bag used in step one of Margaret's mailing system. Private clients of mine get access to a complete "Done for You" system that uses this approach to lock in difficult-to-get appointments.

For those prospects who don't reply, we developed a follow-up letter, to be sent within two business weeks of the first. This one includes an envelope with a bag of shredded dollars from the United States Mint.

The message goes something like this:

I never heard from you after I sent you the bank bag, so I'm sending along a bunch of twenty-dollar bills I put into a shredder in my office to show you how much you're throwing away on your current insurance provider because I haven't negotiated for you.

As step two in Margaret's three-step system, this bag is sent out in a plain, hand-addressed envelope along with a simple letter.

That might seem like a bit of a "bold" approach to take, but results prove that a bold message combined with a powerful visual aid will convert higher than a tame, "professional"-sounding letter.

Finally, if there's no response to the first two mailings, we send out a letter with a fake million-dollar bill attached to the top. The content of the letter is an adaptation of the famous copywriter Gary Halbert's "Dollar-Bill Letter."

It goes something like this:

I've attached a million-dollar bill to this letter for two reasons. One, I needed to get your attention. Two, what I have to share with you is a matter of great financial importance to you and your company's future.

We proceed to bring up our core marketing message again and pull out all the stops in an attempt to get the CEO to set up a fifteen-minute discovery call.

This high-impact, three-step system has helped Margaret fill her calendar with qualified appointments with highly motivated and engaged CEOs, week after week.

Summary

By taking a unique approach to direct mail, you can cut through the noise of "inbox overwhelm" and present a unique, attention-getting message. This strategy works especially well if you're looking to book appointments with people who are hard to reach and who don't respond to e-mail messages.

When you're looking at a market, decide if the cost per appointment would be worth the investment in a 3-D campaign. A word to the wise: Don't dismiss this idea if it costs you a few dollars to mail each piece. Do the math!

If it costs you $2 to mail a piece and you get one appointment for every one hundred you send out, that's a cost of $200 per appointment. Assuming an average closing ratio of 50 percent, it will cost you $400 to close one new client with this method.

Are your commissions greater than $400 per client? If so, then you're already in a positive ROI, not to mention the long-term client commissions and any referrals you might yield from this new relationship.

Let's say an agent pays $2 to $3 per piece and sends several hundred pieces to a targeted list. From that, he may get one client — but that one client transfers hundreds of thousands, even millions, into his management. So he's spending more, but he's getting better clients — and making his money back a hundredfold.

This is a *SHIFT* from the traditional method of "shotgun mailing" — sending ten thousand postcards, one to every house in the seventeen neighborhoods around your office.

"It's not about how much each piece costs," says Travis. "It's about the $20,000 commission from the commercial-lines client, plus his referrals, plus next year's commissions on the deal, plus any additional personal business you write for him as a result. And you got all that from sending a 76¢ piece of mail. Imagine if you spent a bit more."

The Takeaway 👍

- ☐ Make a list of ways you can help clients by using the bank bag/money bag concept (e.g., save money, make money, keep money, etc.).

- ☐ Create an ROI scenario to calculate how many sales you would need to make if each mailing campaign cost you $500.

- ☐ Download the interview I did with Travis Lee to get more in-depth ideas and techniques. It's in the book's Bonus section.

- ☐ Listen to a bonus interview with more strategies at www.TheShiftNation.org

CHAPTER 32

The Secret Behind the Most Innovative Direct-Mail Campaigns in the Industry

"Don't be afraid to give up the good to go for the great."
—John D. Rockefeller

Application: B2B, B2C
Difficulty: Easy
Time to implement: One week
Cost to implement: $2 to $5 a piece

If you've made it this far into the book, you deserve a hearty "congrats"!

Did you know that in 2014, the Pew Research Center reported that nearly a quarter of American adults had not read a single book in the previous year! Incredible! Yet here you are, already in the top percentage, and you've made it through to the twenty-eighth chapter! You, my friend, are a student of the game, and soon to become a master of this profitable craft. You are truly a "*SHIFTer*"!

OK, now back to the goods.

You read about 3-D mail strategies in the last chapter. Sure, it costs more per piece than a traditional flat direct mailing. But as you now understand, all smart insurance and financial marketing strategies are driven by the ROI.

And the key to a high ROI is a highly targeted campaign.

This was the problem facing Marty. He was using the same old referral techniques used by most advisors—until he came across this methodology. Perhaps you are like

Marty was, going from one tactic to another, hopelessly searching seminars, blogs, and magazines for a grain of an idea that could work to attract more ideal clients.

I call this trial-and-error approach "shiny-object marketing." You hear about someone doing something that appears to be working so you immediately drop your plan and chase that "shiny object" down. By trying one new strategy after another, you never complete any of them and your business becomes a fractured collage of half-executed plans that can never give you the consistent, long-term lead generation you need.

In this chapter, we're going to break down a successful direct-mail strategy you can model step by step. I think you'll especially love it because the target audience we present may at first seem like a hard-to-reach one, but eventually proves to be surprisingly simple to nail down if you know where to get the public data.

As you review it, ask yourself, *How can I make a SHIFT from scattered marketing to a consistent marketing plan? What elements from Marty's experience can I use in my agency or financial practice?*

The Agent Who Took the Widow out to Coffee

Marty Higgins, from Pennsylvania, was one agent who understood the *SHIFT* to targeted mailing. When he wanted to get serious about growth, the first thing he did was locate a highly targeted list of his IDEAL prospects.

Have you done this yet? Do you even know who your ideal prospect is?

Marty decided to focus on local recently divorced and widowed women with assets. It was a small list — maybe one hundred to two hundred people. His first letter wasn't three-dimensional at all; it was what Travis refers to as "outrageous mail": a "cup of coffee" offer.

The message went something like:

> *Dear Betty,*
> *It's a bad time. Things are changing. I'd just like to offer you a cup of coffee and a second opinion.*

The envelope came with a coffee stain right on it, so it stood out.

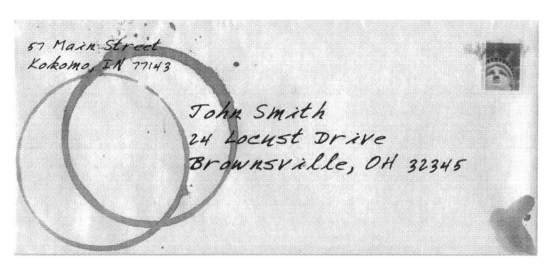

From Coffee Stain to Real Attention-Grabber

For his second mailing, Marty sent "a round tuit" — literally, a little wooden token that said "TUIT" on it. (Get it?)

The letter said:

> *Dear Betty,*
>
> *I sent you that cup-of-coffee letter a few weeks ago. I just wanted to reach out again because maybe you wanted to talk but just didn't get around to it? I thought I'd give you a second opportunity.*

This kind of humorous little pattern interrupt is bound to get a smile from your prospect and forge an emotional connection with you instantly!

The Bug

A few weeks later, Marty sent out a bug.

Not a real bug — a little toy. A cute bug.

This time, the accompanying letter said:

> *Dear Betty,*
>
> *I sent you an offer for a cup of coffee, and then I sent you a round TUIT. This is the last time I'm going to bug you about this — but maybe we can get together for a cup of coffee to get some honest advice about your financial possibilities.*

Marty's ROI

This is a great example of going after a very specific group with a unique approach.

All three steps may have cost Marty $5 per lead. To mail to two hundred people, he spent around $1,000. But because he was marketing to high-net-worth leads, if he netted even one client, he made a profit on the campaign.

And as he got updated lists, he could use the same technique over and over. He didn't have to reinvent the wheel each time.

The Twenty-Seven-Minute Savings Audit

Remember Travis's vinyl bank bag mailing that we talked about in the last chapter? Here's an alternative mail pitch to go with it:

> *Let's sit down for a short, twenty-seven-minute meeting. We'll review your investments and assets. We believe that, based on the information we have, we can save you [X amount of dollars]. And that's why we're sending you this bank bag — for all that money you'll save!*

Note the twenty-seven minutes. It's an odd number, which is another attention-grabber. It's not thirty minutes or half an hour, which sound general and overused. An odd number tells the audience you've planned out your proposal entirely, down the minute.

You may even want to name your system "The Twenty-Seven-Minute Benefits Risk Audit" or "The Twenty-Seven-Minute Profit-Finding Audit."

A Different Take on Part Two of the Mailer

As you'll recall, the second mailer is the shredded money. The accompanying letter might say something like:

> *I'm that guy who sent you the bank bag last week, and promised to save you [X amount of dollars] on your company benefits. But for some reason, you didn't call me to take me up on my Twenty-Seven-Minute Benefits Risk Audit (or whatever you're calling it).*
>
> *The only thing I can imagine is that you're not interested in saving money. So I took a couple of $20 bills and put them through the shredder, just to show you how much money you're wasting.*

The more direct you can be, the better.

The Fake Million-Dollar Bill

Next comes that fake million. Perhaps the letter accompanying it might say:

> *I hope you remember me. I'm the guy who sent you the bank bag and the shredded money. This time, I've sent you a million-dollar bill. I've done that because I really believe that we can save you some money. In the long run, over the life of your company, it could be millions of dollars!*

A campaign like this might cost you $10 to $12 per lead. Sending to list of one hundred would cost you $1,200.

But if you get one client out of it, you're already ahead of the game.

Summary

Even with a difficult-to-find market, you can get lists of people who fit your exact target profile. The SRDS is a great place to start to find targets within your precise demographics (Google it).

By taking an ROI-based approach to your marketing and avoiding the "shiny-object chasing" that most advisors engage in, you'll be able to implement a strong, consistent lead-generation funnel.

Using unconventional methods of which most advisors aren't aware — such as creative calls to action and attention grabbing 3-D direct-mail pieces — you outpace the competition for those high-net-worth clients.

What offer could you develop using some of the ideas we offered in this chapter? What kind of positive impact might you create by adding an inventive new element to your marketing mix?

The Takeaway

☐ Determine your specific ideal-client profile and then target them creatively.

☐ Develop a unique direct-mail strategy such as the one Marty used. Build the theme around the area of most concern to your prospects.

☐ Use the three-step system to market to these prospects, deploying these formulas exactly, or some version of them.

CHAPTER 33

The Surprising Way to Grab the Most Market Share for the Least Amount of Money

"Innovation distinguishes between a leader and a follower."
—Steve Jobs

You know those commercials for insurance companies such as GEICO, State Farm, and MassMutual? Have you ever watched one and wondered which works better for insurance products: advertising on TV or advertising on the Internet?

Well, you might be surprised at the answer.

I'd like to start off this chapter by sharing some powerful insights that will help you *SHIFT* your thinking and open your mind to some more marketing ideas that might serve you.

But instead of just telling you a few anecdotes this time, I'm going to provide you with some conclusive, third-party data that validates my theories and strategies. That way, if you have to convince someone on your team to approve the use of any of these tactics, you'll have some great data to back you up.

A word to the wise: some of the data in this chapter concerns some multibillion-dollar firms whose daily marketing budget exceeds the yearly expenditure of most agents and advisors. Not to worry! The great news is that these principles can be successfully scaled down to apply to smaller agencies. (I've included plenty of great case studies and examples you can learn from throughout this book.)

Ready? OK, let's dive in!

Digital Trumps Personal

In 2014, TransUnion found that 44 percent of auto-insurance shoppers look at just one quote before buying. And a complementary study by Rocket Fuel shows that 55 percent of people who *start* their journey online end up *buying* online.

They also found that buyers first discover auto insurance in one of two ways:

- From someone they know (41 percent)
- From advertisements (25 percent)

Why You Must Be Online

So what does this mean for you?

Regardless of what you're selling, it's extremely important to have *some* sort of online presence.

After all, more than half of all consumers — 55 percent — research providers online. And in the end, no matter how great a personal recommendation they receive, 39 percent of consumers rely on a digital source in making their final decision.

Think about that. **More than *one-third* of all people who buy an insurance policy make their FINAL choice based on something they see on the Internet!**

So, the question is . . .

What type of information does your website, your blog, your Facebook page, and your LinkedIn profile offer in order to grab that 40 percent of the market?

Why You Don't Need a Million-Dollar Budget

A quick point before we continue: as we discuss these studies, you might think, *Well, I don't have the budget of GEICO or State Farm.*

Well, that's OK. In fact, it's great — because it means you can be smarter about your advertising expenditure. You see, many of the giant firms have ad programs SO large that they don't keep track of the minutia, the smallest pieces of the campaign.

When you have a smaller budget and you're marketing on just one platform or in just one market — or both — you can micromanage your metrics. Rest assured, we can take what the big boys are doing and easily adapt it for our own use.

The Number One Factor in Gaining a Competitive Edge

Back to the Rocket Fuel study, where we learned that nearly half of all people look at just one quote before buying. Well, 15 percent *don't even request a quote* before they decide to buy a policy. How can that be?

It's because of a phenomenon called "top of mind."

Top of mind simply means that your brand — your agency name and what people associate with it — comes to mind first and most strongly at the point when a buyer is pulling out his credit card. Top-of-mind awareness is *so strong* that it can almost predict your ultimate market share.

How to Stay Top of Mind

So, needless to say, top of mind is where you want to be.

In the auto-insurance world, the two major brands that dominate top-of-mind awareness are GEICO and State Farm. Here's a screenshot from the study that shows the top-of-mind awareness and total ad spend for the top ten auto insurers in 2013 and in 2014.

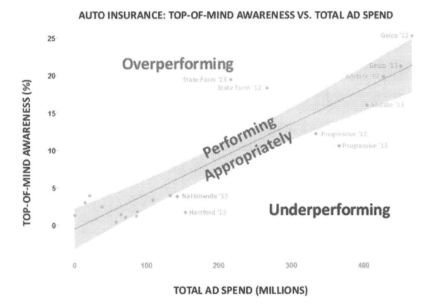

Source: Rocket Fuel Top-of-Mind Awareness Insurance Study
http://www.slideshare.net/Rocketfuelinc/top-of-mindinsurancewebinarpresentation

Anyone within the gray bar is getting a great return on investment. Anyone *below* the gray bar is underperforming, or not getting his money's worth. And anyone *above* the gray bar is overperforming.

Notice that GEICO is at the top right of the chart, but State Farm has considerably high awareness for the amount of money that it's spending.

Dig a little deeper and you'll find out that, while GEICO spends more money than State Farm on TV ads, which can lead to oversaturation, State Farm invests more in the *digital* realm.

Looking at this next chart, you can see that State Farm also spends more in the display-ad channel.

The Secret to an Outstanding Return on Investment

It turns out that display ads — those little banners that show up on websites and Facebook and LinkedIn feeds — are *nine* times more effective than television ads when it comes to generating top-of-mind awareness.

So how can you get the same results as the big brands while spending just $20 or $30 a day?

Facebook.

We'll get into more specifics as to HOW to create a conversion-crushing Facebook campaign in the next chapter. But for now, you should know that this is how the big boys are doing it, and how you can do it too — for a fraction of the cost.

Summary

Since so *many* people make insurance-purchasing decisions based on it, it's imperative that you design campaigns that build top-of-mind awareness.

A great place to do this among your desired market is Facebook.

The Takeaway 👍

☐ Be prepared to think about ways you can develop top-of-mind awareness for your insurance or financial product.

☐ Pay particular attention to the ideas and examples in this book that may inspire you to create this in your market.

CHAPTER 34

Creating a Killer Facebook Ad Campaign 101

"It is better to fail in originality than to succeed in imitation."
- Herman Melville

Application: B2B, B2C
Difficulty: Advanced
Time to implement: One hour
Cost to implement: $25 a day

Marketing on Facebook can be a daunting and intimidating experience. Should you "friend" your ideal clients and engage with them? Is it better to put ads in their streams? Do both?

In this chapter we're going to discuss one very specific and actionable *SHIFT* to Facebook marketing. What I think you'll like about it is that it doesn't take hours to develop, doesn't require you to think of funny or shareable content, and doesn't involve racking your brain to create something "viral."

It's a simple and straightforward strategy that will expose your message to your ideal market and present a relevant message that drives them to take action.

My prediction is that once you read this chapter, your fears about Facebook will melt, you'll approach the medium with more confidence, and you'll want to jump right in!

Want a fast and easy way to get started with Facebook? Wonder if there is a successful model out there you can swipe and deploy? Read on.

The Commercial-Lines Start-up—Facebook Style

When Kent started his commercial-lines agency, he faced several options.

He could call everyone he knew, book some appointments, and write some business. From there, he could ask for referrals. Once those dried out, he could start looking for local networking groups or associations to join to make new connections. That's what most principals of a start-up would do.

Another option would be to invest tens of thousands of dollars in expensive branding and a corporate-looking website presence, then sit back and hope it will drive business.

Or, he could attempt to poach producers from rival agencies with attractive sign-on bonuses and hope they'll bring their business over to his firm. (And that the legal problems that would no doubt ensue could be kept to a minimum.)

Kent did none of those. Instead, he turned to Facebook and used a unique technique I'm going to outline for you in glaring detail in this chapter.

This strategy is so powerful that within eighteen months of consistently using it, Kent's little three-person team sold its entire book for a million dollars — cash!

Target Your Audience

The first step in this plan — as in so many others outlined in this book — is to identify your IDEAL client. (Why do I say this over and over? Because it absolutely WORKS!)

In Kent's case, the firm had a great product for apartment-building owners that the market could not compete with. So he decided to go after real-estate investors and use Facebook to target them. His first move was to find people who had had "liked" groups related to the subject, e.g., Robert Kiyosaki, Dean Graziosi, House Flipping, etc.

In your case, you might decide to target specific ZIP codes to reach your precise target, perhaps combined with a certain level of net worth.

Let's say your agency wants to target high-net-worth consumers who are good prospects for personal insurance or investment products.

You can target people within the city of Chicago, for example . . .

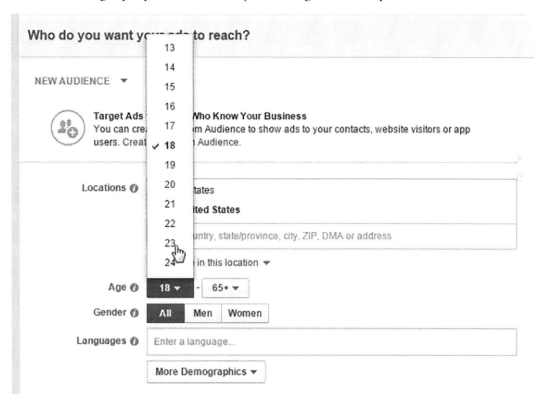

. . . who are between the ages of forty-five and sixty-five-plus.

Now, let's look at some ways of narrowing your target even further.

You can target people by relationship status (single, married, divorced, widowed) . . .

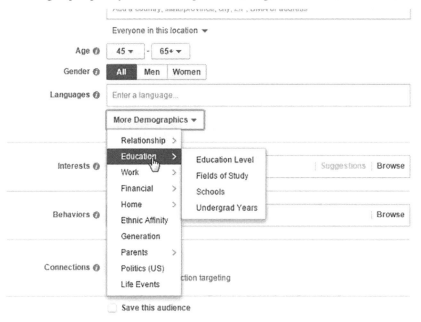

. . . or by education level, field of study, schools attended, or simply their number of undergraduate years.

You can even target people who work at specific companies, hold specific job titles, work in particular industries, or at certain kinds of offices.

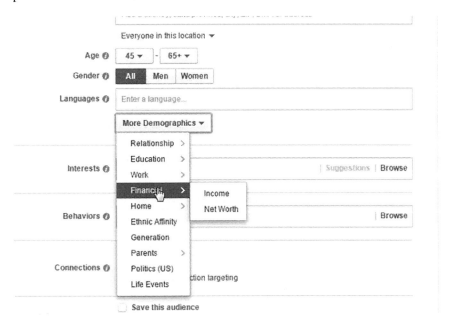

And, significantly, you can look at their net worth. In this example, I chose somebody with a net worth of $100,000.

After applying sufficient narrowing criteria, you'll have a group of people who compose your target market.

As you continue to refine your demographics, you'll see the number of users you reach diminish. This is a good thing, because it means your ad is highly targeted.

Keep in mind, however, that when you're testing ads, you don't want to use too many different variables. Test within just one category or another, so you can determine for sure which types of ads convert best.

Next, I want to find out what type of homes my target prospects own.

I am interested only in people with a home value of $100,000+.

This should be really interesting to you if you sell products tied to life events:

You can target people who have an anniversary within the next thirty days, people who are away from their family or their hometown, people who are about to start a new job (a great opportunity to review their life insurance), people starting a new relationship, or those who got engaged in the last year, three months, or six months . . .

. . . even people who have recently gotten married!

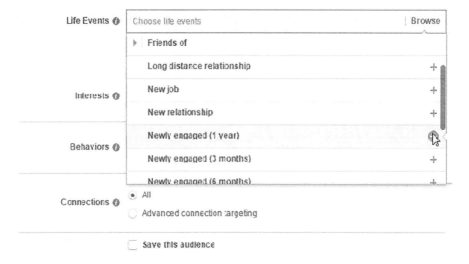

If you are interested in health-insurance prospects, you can add a fitness-and-wellness component to your parameters, i.e., those who have wealth, a home, *and an interest in fitness.*

Then you can roll out a group of ads specifically tailored to those looking to save money on health insurance.

One of my clients on the East Coast uses shopping behavior as a criterion, targeting those who like expensive brands, such as Prada, Coach, and Mercedes-Benz. Then, he creates specific ads about investing and getting better-quality coverage on home and auto.

For those selling auto insurance, Facebook can be a real boon.

Did you know that Facebook integrates with DLX, a massive source of information on all of the cars in the United States? This means you can even target people who are in the market for certain vehicles!

So, let's say you want to rule out all those who are looking for an economy vehicle and reach only those in the market for a luxury automobile. Thanks to Facebook, you can do that!

You can target people who are new to car shopping. You can target by vehicle age and price. You can target people who have purchased motorcycles, if you offer that coverage. You can even target people who are receptive to online auto-insurance offers.

You really can't get more detailed than that.

The Ideal Budget

Believe it or not, you can get started on Facebook with an ad budget of just $5 per day. In the beginning, I recommend $20 a day just to generate a bit more traffic. But if you'd rather go slowly, start with $5 or $10. Then, as you start optimizing your ads, you can ramp up from there.

Five Steps to the Perfect Facebook Ad

Now that you have a handle on targeting and budget, what should your advertisement *look* like?

A recent Rocket Fuel study showed that the following triggers helped to INCREASE conversions.

1. Don't mention pricing. Insurance ads that don't mention price have slightly higher conversion rates (10 percent higher) than those that do.

2. Add a face to the ad. This could be yourself or a stock photo. When used in the right way, a human face made conversions rise by 200 percent.

3. Choose images that show the desired results. In our own tests, we found that the highest conversion rates came from showing what our product or service could help the customer achieve. So if you're targeting investment and retirement products, you might want to show a couple in their late fifties or sixties embracing and smiling. This will tend to convert more than, say, a shot of an older couple poring over documents or looking at a laptop.

4. Test red versus blue. That same Rocket Fuel study showed that ads with red or blue backgrounds had a 20 percent higher conversion rate than those using any other color. They also had higher click-through rates.

5. Use a "call to action" button. Buttons that say "Apply Now" have the highest conversion rates of all.

Where Should the Clicks Go?

When building your Facebook campaign, it's important to give special consideration to WHERE you're going to send your traffic. This might surprise you, but the worst place you can send prospects — the place with the LOWEST conversion level — is the home page of your website.

That's because, in your ad, you've promised a specific benefit or action, e.g., get a quote, download this report, watch a video, etc. To keep your cost per lead low and your ads as effective as possible, direct your traffic to a landing page where the only action they can take is the next step in the process.

We'll discuss landing pages in another chapter. For now, just be aware that you should be sending traffic directly to a quote page where they can download a report or take the next step in the plan.

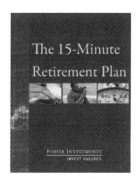

FISHER INVESTMENTS®

15-Minute Retirement Plan

Get your FREE copy of The 15-Minute Retirement Plan

No cost or obligation beyond completing a short request form and survey.

Running out of money in retirement is one of the biggest risks investors face. Working your whole life to gather enough wealth for retirement, only to realize too late it's just not enough, can be devastating. This guide addresses important issues investors face in retirement, including:

· How long your portfolio will actually need to provide for you.
· How cash distributions and inflation impact your portfolio.
· Why you need to establish a primary investment objective.
· *And much more!*

Click here - It's FREE!

* This offer contains timely information.

Norton SECURED
powered by Symantec

Fisher Investments | 5525 NW Fisher Creek Dr. | Camas, WA 98607 | 1-800-587-5506 | inquiry@fi.com
Your privacy is extremely important to us. Click here to view our Privacy Policy.
Investments in securities involve the risk of loss.
©2015 Fisher Investments. All rights reserved.

*The landing page for one of the most prolific investment marketers online,
Fisher Investments uses a simple call to action with no other links, to help prospects
move to the next step in their funnel.*

Summary

In this chapter, we looked at the basics of Facebook marketing. You learned how targeted you can be and exactly what kind of ad to run — ads that use the five highest-converting elements.

Finally, we discussed the best place to send your traffic if you want to keep your cost per lead low and your conversions high.

What market could you be targeting on Facebook to start testing? What valuable incentive could you offer that would make your target audience want to click on your ad and take action?

The Takeaway 👍

☐ Set up a free Facebook account to start placing ads.

☐ Choose the areas where you would like to place your ads.

☐ Define your target audience.

☐ Design an ad based on the best practices above.

☐ Launch your campaign and test it for a week to see how it performs.

CHAPTER 35

How to Fill a Social Security Seminar for Just $20.19 per Person

"I keep on making what I can't do yet in order to learn to be able to do it."
—Vincent van Gogh

Application: B2B, B2C
Difficulty: Moderate
Time to implement: Two hours
Cost to implement: $10 per day, minimum

Seminar marketing can be an effective way to sift an audience for the right prospects. However, it can be brutally expensive, especially if you're paying for the meal.

It's not uncommon for financial advisors to pay $3,000 to $8,000 to fill a room of thirty prospects — with a cost per attendee upwards of $200. This is because most advisors use only ONE method to fill up a seminar.

But with the advent of geographic and demographic targeting on YouTube and Facebook, it's possible to supplement your direct-response efforts with digital marketing techniques.

In this chapter you'll marvel at the incredibly inexpensive way you can generate highly qualified leads in your precise market for a fraction of what you'd pay using direct-response methods.

The Incredible Facebook-Seminar Marketing Hack

Nelson is a client of mine in Hawaii. He's an affable, gregarious, and amazing human being; to know him is to love him. On our consulting video sessions, he starts off with a warm "Aloha!" And, as a Million Dollar Round Table member, he's experienced years of our seminar marketing techniques, many of which have helped him build his practice.

Like most advisors, Nelson's typical strategy when I first met him was to work with his FMO to market seminars using direct-response postcards. This resulted in a cost per attendee of more than $200.

We helped him try something different — and his results were groundbreaking. The important *SHIFT* we made was to supplement his offline postcard seminar-marketing technique with a complementary *online* marketing strategy.

Nelson started using Facebook and YouTube ads to promote his seminars right along with his regular direct-response tactics. So, if you were within his desired ZIP code and looking at a video on YouTube, you would see Nelson's ad before your own video.

Within Facebook, we selected a custom audience of his ideal targets who would see a small ad directly in their Facebook stream. These were people living within fifteen miles of his ZIP code, over the age of fifty-five, and with a net worth of over $200,000. That gave Nelson thirty thousand people to market to on a small test budget of $25 a day.

We were a bit late running the ad due to technical issues with Facebook, but we were able to start five days before the event — definitely a short window of time.

The cost of the ad for five days, at a cap of $25 per day, was $125.

Here's the ad that we ran, which, incidentally, converted at 312 percent higher than industry standards. (That means you should swipe this ad!)

The ad our team used to promote a local financial-planning event.

Here Are the Results

For a Tuesday seminar, we began marketing on Sunday and had two sign-ups and no show-ups.

That didn't surprise us. But it was a good test piece to see whether people were at least willing to sign up for a local event they'd learned about on Facebook a mere day before it was to occur!

For a Saturday seminar, we began marketing on the previous Sunday (giving us five days total, since we didn't market on the day of the event).

We had twelve sign-ups. And a whopping 50 percent attendance rate!

A 50 percent attendance rate with minimal marketing via a Facebook ad? That's phenomenal! And since six people showed up, our cost per attendee was just $20.19 — 958 percent LOWER than industry standards from traditional postcards!

All of this was because Nelson made the *SHIFT* from purely offline to a hybrid of digital and offline. Isn't this is a beautiful example of how a new way of marketing can complement a traditional model? What hybrid possibilities can you take advantage of in your own marketing to drastically reduce your costs and open up a whole new market?

Another benefit we enjoyed, though we couldn't track it statistically, was the potentially increased response rate from the postcards — because people received the postcard PLUS saw the ad online. Did this influence attendance? The test was too small to tell, but it is a bedrock principle of marketing that multiple contact points can only help conversions.

Offering Value to Get More Appointments

As a bonus, here's something else Nelson tried:

At the end of one seminar, he offered a special report worth $500 to every attendee who made an appointment with him. In another, he conducted a drawing for a book on retirement. If you requested a meeting, you got to enter the drawing. With these two simple strategies, Nelson saw 54 percent of his attendees sign up for a meeting at one seminar, and 50 percent at the other.

The industry average? Just 30 percent.

What ideas does this spark in you? What could you add to your marketing mix that could make your current lead-generation efforts even more powerful?

Summary

Nelson's inspiring story is a wonderful example of how you can blend digital with traditional, offline marketing strategies that are already working. Though many of my documented breakthroughs have been in the digital space, I've never advocated throwing out the old. As you start to think like a strategic marketer, you know that it's about using all of the available assets at your disposal to reap windfalls of profits wherever you look.

In this case, taking a modern twist on an old problem — filling seminars — led to an unprecedented breakthrough of hyper-targeting. And that led to an almost 1,000 percent reduction in cost per lead!

What *SHIFT* in your thinking about marketing could you make *right now* that would open up doors of opportunity?

The Takeaway 👍

☐ Be willing to try new marketing methods, or supplement methods that are working with new ones. Test the possibilities and see what happens.

☐ YouTube and Facebook ads work well to supplement a direct-response seminar marketing model, if you have enough lead time.

☐ Test different formats, media, and lead times.

CHAPTER 36

"Angry Birds" Marketing: How Embedded Content Discovery Can Gain You Millions More Impressions a Month

"All men can see these tactics whereby I conquer,
but what none can see is the strategy out of which victory is evolved."
—Sun Tzu

Application: B2B, B2C
Difficulty: Advanced
Time to implement: One day
Cost to implement: $100 to start

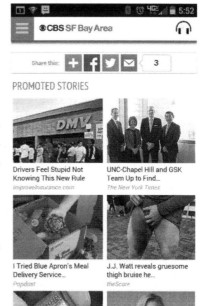

One day, I was in San Diego for a conference and started browsing on my phone for the news. After reading an article related to the economy, the following promoted stories came up.

Guess which one caught my eye?

OK, I do admit the thigh bruise did grab me first.

But then, I saw the incredibly clever headline in the upper left, used to market car insurance.

"Drivers Feel Stupid Not Knowing This New Rule"

First, the marketer in me got really curious. My marketing "antennae" are always up, alert to finding curious ways that people are using marketing to drive insurance and financial sales.

Then, the clever headline smacked me right in the head. *BAM!*

Hats off to the well-written headline. It makes you feel as if you're missing out a simple trick, doesn't it?

You might be wondering, *How do people get their little ads there, in the news sections of major websites? And, can it be done affordably?*

Yes! Enter Outbrain.

The Beauty of Content Discovery Networks

Content Discovery Networks are platforms that have negotiated space on the websites of the major news networks of the world. Instead of placing direct ads for products and services, however, these networks places content on such sites as CNN, The Wall Street Journal, TIME, and The New York Times.

You'll see them under the heading "Promoted Stories" on websites and mobile apps.

More than ninety thousand blogs use Outbrain to serve up relevant recommendations to readers — more than fifty billion of them — per month.

A screenshot shows the promoted stories distributed by Outbrain on CNN.com.

If your ideal audience is reading a story, services such as Outbrain can then offer them a relevant story — your story — hoping they'll click on it after reading the news.

If they do click on your story, Outbrain charges you a small fee, and that visitor ends up reading a well-written article on your website that compels them to take action when they're done. That action could be to fill out a form, download a report, request an insurance quote, or take another step in the process of purchasing your services.

It's Simple to Get Started

For just $100, you can start an account with Outbrain, write up a short story, and then place it on content networks.

Campaign Name		Status	Start Date	End Date	CPC	Budget	Spent Budget
Outbrain Blog - Earned Media Tips	▲	Off-Air	09/01/13	09/30/13	$ 0.25	$ 200 daily	$ 0.00
Outbrain_Hispanic_English		On-Air	03/15/13	Always on	$ 0.35	$ 50 daily	$ 5.60
Outbrain_Hispanic_Spanish		Off-Air	03/15/13	Always on	$ 0.5	$ 10 daily	$ 0.00
Outbrain_PuertoRico		Off-Air	03/15/13	Always on	$ 0.5	$ 10 daily	$ 0.00
Outbrain_Spanish3rdParty		Off-Air	06/28/13	Always on	$ 0.2	$ 10 daily	$ 10.00
Selfserve_2013selfserve		On-Air	11/28/12	Always on	$ 0.1	$ 50 daily	$ 49.00

Outbrain's dashboard is easy to use and helps you discover where your audience is hanging out online.

Instead of your target audience clicking to a lead-generation form, they are clicking over to your story — so you need to create a well-written article that compels them to take action and request a quote.

Optimus Prime and State Farm: Roll Out!

This next strategy is far too expensive for the average agent, but it's a great illustration of how far you can go with embedded content and cash in on the digital trend.

Not too long ago, State Farm made a major media buy. They embedded themselves in one of the hottest mobile-app games on the market: Angry Birds Transformers.

In the game, you play the role of a Transformer, out there battling the evil Deceptihogs (No, that was not a typo).

The game is simple: Try to avoid getting shot at by the Deceptihogs while taking down their shields. Since you're constantly taking on enemy fire, you can acquire special shields that temporarily protect your player so you can make it that much further.

State Farm saw an opportunity to tap into the massive millennial market *by being a part of the game itself.* They did this by branding the shields with their logo, for a clever promotional tie-in!

Here's a screenshot to show you what I mean:

Screenshot from the Angry Birds Transformers app, showing State Farm sponsorship.

Notice the three circular icons at the top left? Branded. And, though it may be hard to see, the shield generator gauge at the bottom has the State Farm logo on it as well.

Besides the great branding exposure for State Farm, on an emotional level, the player now associates the company with *protection.*

Well played, State Farm. Well played.

Summary

In this chapter, you learned how Content Discovery Networks work and how to use them to drive traffic to your offer by embedding content into the major media networks targeted to your ideal audience. This can easily be set up with an account with a provider like Outbrain.

We also reviewed an advanced method used by State Farm to embed their brand into a game — and the lives of millennials — to grow its market share.

What opportunities have you missed out on by not having your content online for your target audience to discover?

The Takeaway

- ☐ To boost traffic to your lead page, study what others players are doing in your space and then write a short, compelling story that speaks to your target audience.

- ☐ Add a page to your website with the story.

- ☐ Set up a small $100 account on Outbrain.com.

- ☐ Test out sending traffic to your page and study the conversions to see if this initiative works within your ROI model.

CHAPTER 37

Write a Book and Profit: Four Ways to Become a Published Author and Instantly Boost Your Credibility

"The more scared we are of a work or calling,
the more sure we can be that we have to do it."
—Steven Pressfield

Premium Sold: Excess of $10 million
Difficulty: Advanced
Time to implement: One week to four months
Cost to implement: $200 to $20,000

Writing a book can be one of the most daunting tasks an insurance or financial advisor can take on. Sitting down and writing hundreds (or even dozens) of pages is the LEAST favorite activity of most people.

A recent study showed that 81 percent of Americans feel they have book "inside of them" that they could write, but the VAST majority won't ever try it.

Prolific author and professor at Northwestern University Joseph Epstein aptly put it this way: "Without attempting to overdo the drama of the difficulty of writing, to be in the middle of composing a book is almost always to feel oneself in a state of confusion, doubt, and mental imprisonment, with an accompanying intense wish that one worked instead at bricklaying."

This fourteen-time author may be right — but I'd still like to share with you a few unique strategies for writing a book with a minimum amount of pain. You'll also find some key reasons why you SHOULD consider either writing a book — or having one written for you.

Why Every Agent and Advisor Should Have a Book

The Oakley Institute once interviewed affluent investors to find out what qualities they associate with a successful advisor or agent. Thirty-seven percent respected designations such as CFP, MBA, etc. Thirty-two percent — nearly the same amount — placed more value on personal presence and people skills.

So, how can you enhance your personal presence when meeting with a prospect? By having a book with your name on it.

The Thud Factor

Imagine walking into your ideal client's office. After exchanging pleasantries, you pull out your business card and hand it over. Then you chitchat for a while about the weather, the nice pictures on the wall, business . . . the usual.

Your prospect wants to start the meeting, but just as he opens his mouth, you gently and respectfully hold up your hand and say, "Sorry to cut you off there, Jim. I completely forgot; I brought you a gift!"

Then you reach down into your briefcase, fake rummaging around for a few seconds to build the suspense, and slowly pull out a book.

You gently place it so that one end touches the table first, and then drop the other end gently so it makes a satisfying *THUD!* as it lands.

That is what we call the "thud factor."

WOW.

Only a book can give you that impressive thud factor. It shows that you have not only an incredible personal presence, but a *professional* presence as well. The presence of an expert.

Which would you rather leave behind: a business card . . . or a book?

Other Credibility-Boosting Techniques

Even if you don't meet with people in person, it's worth having a book with your name on it. Imagine the power of adding a book credit to your LinkedIn profile or Facebook page: "Author of *Demystifying Annuities: Seven Secrets Your Advisor Doesn't Want You to Know*" or "*Author of Switch: How CEOs Are Switching to Self-Funded Plans to Preserve Profits and Grow Their Companies FAST.*"

Or imagine what it would sound like to have someone reference your book in a web conference, as part of your introduction. The gravitas and power of this are priceless.

How could your seminars or sales conversations change by saying, "One of the things that I mention in my book . . ." or, "One of the things I wrote an entire chapter on . . ." or, "You know what? That's a great question. In fact, it comes up so often that I devoted an entire chapter to it in my book . . ."?

Getting Over the Intimidation Factor

But, as I said, the thought of writing a book can be very intimidating, which is why so few people attempt it.

There are lots of ways you can create a book. You can even have someone else do it for you and still benefit from the credibility and presence it lends you everywhere you go.

Let me just give you a quick way to think about writing a book. (Even if you've already got one under your belt, it's never too late to try something different.)

I should know. At first, I thought I had to write a magnum opus. The Bible of insurance and financial marketing. But I was overwhelmed at the amount of time and effort that would take, and a one- or two-month project turned into one or two years.

So, I changed my focus.

Instead of thinking of my book as the *Great Insurance and Financial Marketing Book*, I decided it would be my FIRST book — which just happened to be "great." In my first book, I just wanted my readers to get to know me better, while I provided them with a lot of value.

You're reading that book now.

So what's the lesson?

Stop imagining that you need to write the *ultimate* book. Instead, think of it as the ultimate book you're writing *now*. It's not about getting the book perfect. It's about making progress toward getting it done.

Version *One* is better than Version *None*.

If you get your content to 80 percent, get it out the door. In fact, if you always focus on 80 percent, you'll get things done much faster than your competitors, who are slaving away over their final versions. They may never get anything out the door, while you'll have a credible book in the marketplace.

So . . . how can you add a book credit to your resume?

Method One: The Simple Journalism Formula for Writing Your Own Book

The most obvious way to produce a book is to write it yourself, and I'm going to give you a simple framework to get you started. It makes use of the old journalism nugget, "Who, Where, When, What, Why, and How."

First, pick a theme. Let's say it's about life insurance.

The first section of your book can be called, "Who Needs Life Insurance?" The next section might be the opposite of that same question: "Who *Doesn't* Need Life Insurance?

Then you move on to the "where."

Where is life insurance applicable?

Follow that with the negative: Where *wouldn't* you use life insurance?

Next, you tackle the "when."

When is life insurance especially valuable?

When is it *not* valuable?

What is life insurance?

What is life insurance *not*?

Why should you have life insurance?

Why *shouldn't* you have life insurance?

And finally, **how** does life insurance work?

How *doesn't* life insurance work?

If you don't want to write it, just speak your answers into the free MP3 recorder found on your smartphone and send it to someone online to transcribe. Transcription rates tend to be around $0.75 to $1.00 a minute. You can smooth it out and tinker with it once you have it on paper.

Method Two: Hire a Pro to Write It for You

There's a ghostwriter for every budget. My good friend Michael Levin is a *New York Times* best-selling author who has ghostwritten dozens of books for financial professionals. You can find him at www.advisorghost.com (mention me and this book, and they'll give you a special "insider pricing" model).

BOOK BONUS: I've got a wonderful interview with New York Times best-selling author Michael Levin that you can access in the Members area of www.Theshiftnation.org.

Michael told me a story about a financial advisor who was really struggling to make ends meet. She felt that if she could put together a book about the importance of investing, it would help her with her affluent target market in California.

She scrounged up some money from savings and borrowed a little from her friends and family, and hired Michael to write a book for her. Within just six months, she had snagged several new affluent clients. Within a year, her life had completely turned around. She had made six figures in commissions in just that first twelve months.

Clients who are part of my higher-level programs can have an entire book written for them as part of the program, so their process is entirely painless and worry-free. Their ideas are all they need to contribute.

The Ghostwriting Process: What to Expect

Writing with a ghostwriter is fairly simple.

Most ghostwriters follow a template or formula. You can meet with him in person or, more typically, via Skype or over the phone. He asks you a series of questions and records the interview.

Then, he transcribes the conversation and edits the transcript so that it reads like a book. The following week, he might interview you again with some follow-up questions. Again, he records what you say, transcribes it, and edits it.

The entire process takes about six to eight weeks and includes as many interviews as necessary to get the whole thing done to your satisfaction. Once a draft is completed, the ghostwriter shares it with you for your approval or changes.

A ghostwriter can cost anywhere from $2,000 all the way up to $30,000. As with anything in life, you get what you pay for. If you're looking for lower-cost ghostwriters, try Elance. When you post your project there, be sure to put "ghostwriter" and "book" in the headline so you can quickly attract people with relevant experience.

I've found freelancers on Elance who will write a book for just $5,000, but if you want to work with someone who has vast experience in writing more complex business books, you can expect to pay between $30,000 and $120,000.

Self-Publishing and How Many Books to Print?

Most ghostwriters have access to self-publishing houses, so they can help with that as well. There are various outlets that can help you to self-publish. Once your book is ready, many of them provide you with a link for your website, and when somebody orders the book, they print it on demand. That way, you're not stuck with a garage full of books.

Createspace.com, for example, can print, bind, and ship your books in quantities as small as one copy.

I do recommend that you have at least twenty-five books on hand at all times, so you can use them in client meetings and appointments. It's also good to have a few available to mail to people interested in doing business with you.

Method Three: The Power of Many—Collaborating on a Group Book

You could also try writing a group book with people who have similar businesses and target markets. This is very common in some industries.

Basically, each of you writes or dictates a chapter. Then, the chapters are pulled together into a book. Certain services will even help you co-write books with established authors. In that case, you can leverage the celebrity appeal of your big-name co-author. Something like this can start at around $5,000.

The process here is very similar to that of a straight ghostwriting project. You submit to a one-hour interview and somebody else writes your chapter. Then, you can review it and give your final approval.

Method Four: Pull Together Your Own Group Book with Other Professionals

You can even organize something like this yourself. What other businesses, consultants, and advisors serve your ideal clientele?

For example, say you service small businesses.

You can reach out to CPAs, tax attorneys, lawyers, insurance agents, marketing consultants, outsourced HR services, printers, graphic designers, office-supply companies, building-maintenance companies, employee-training organizations, food-delivery services that handle company lunches, hotels that host events and conferences, travel agencies, and the list goes on and on.

Organize the project with three to ten other businesses in your city. Ultimately, each business owner can promote the book. If each of them has, let's say, one thousand people on his mailing list, that's ten thousand new potential clients to whom you will have access.

Not only that. You are positioning yourself as the co-author of a book that helps small business owners succeed. Also, since you organized the project, you can make sure you're the only contributing advisor targeting small-business owners.

Keep It Simple: Why Short Books Are Hot

Finally, you could simply shoot for a short book — the kind that matches the way people read today. Especially busy people.

Did you know that on Amazon there's a category of books that can be read in under two hours? This is one of the fastest-growing categories of Kindle authorship.

You can find a writer on Upwork.com, Scripted.com, or WriterAccess.com, all marketplaces of thousands of writers specifically looking to write short books or articles. It takes about a week to write a short book, so you can get it out faster. Usually, the writer can do most of his or her research online.

To aid in the process, you can Google a few terms, such as "How to invest wisely," "Tips for reducing your insurance costs," or "HR strategies for the Affordable Care Act." Send the writer the links and a rough outline for how the book should be developed.

Smart Titles: How to Come Up with a Book Title That Sells

So how can you use your short book to generate leads and earn a secondary income stream?

First, head over to Google AdWords Keyword Planner tool at

https://adwords.google.com/KeywordPlanner.

Think about the keywords people might use to search for your products and services and research them on Google, using the Keyword Planner. If you title your book using those keywords, you can get it ranked on one of the first pages of Google.

*A screenshot of the free Google AdWords Keyword Planner tool you can use
to determine the best title for your book.*

For instance, if "retire early" is a frequently searched term, you could name your book:

How to Retire Early

Where to Retire Early

The Cost of Retiring Early

Retire Early: Seven Strategies for Retiring Faster Than Your Friends and Living the Life of Your Dreams

Notice how your keywords show up in each of those titles?

Google also loves to recommend Amazon links because they are so popular, so it is more likely to promote a book on the Kindle marketplace than a book you post on your own website.

Summary

Having a book can be a massive credibility builder and an excellent way to help drive your market preeminence. Since very few agents and advisors have a book today, you're distinction and credibility will soar with one of these bad boys under your belt.

The idea of having to sit down at your computer and write out every word of your book is old school. By employing one of many ghostwriters or a simple "Five Ws" strategy, you can have a book written for you in as little as one week. Naming your book is an important part of your strategy to attract more of the market you're targeting.

What could happen to your business if you had a book written with your name on it? How cool would it be to open every meeting with prospects who know they are in the presence of a published author?

The Takeaway

- ☐ Write a book yourself using the simple formula above and your expertise.
- ☐ Hire a ghostwriter to put together a book.
- ☐ Collaborate on a group book with other professionals targeting the same audience.
- ☐ Write a short book.
- ☐ When coming up with titles, use Google AdWords to research frequently used terms in your market.

CHAPTER 38

How to Grow Your Lead Database by 1,500 Percent with the Value-Added Approach

*"We cannot solve our problems with the same
thinking we used when we created them."*
–Albert Einstein

Application: B2B, B2C
Difficulty: Moderate
Time to implement: Two to four weeks
Cost to implement: Optional cost of virtual-meeting tools ($99 month)

We're small-business owners. Most of us operate on a shoestring budget. This can sometimes make marketing feel like an uphill battle. But really, it's an opportunity to get creative.

I once worked at a start-up software company with a sixty-prospect database. We had to look at the fastest, simplest, easiest, and most affordable ways to reach others. Here's one strategy that worked especially well for us. And while you're in insurance, not software, it will work for you, too.

It's all built on the most affordable medium of all: e-mail.

Consider your target audience and how you can provide them with value. Then look to entities that can connect you with your target audience. In our case, our target market was insurance agents and our ideal referral source was carriers.

If you're targeting high-net-worth individuals, tax attorneys might be a good source for you — or CPAs. You get the idea.

Create something valuable that props up the referral source *and* its clients — your prospects. Offer to feature one of those clients in a webinar, white paper, or report.

Have the client talk about how to tackle a major issue facing his market. Then, invite the referral source to distribute the report.

We did this with carriers. We highlighted their top brokers and how they were achieving success. Within sixty days, we had developed five partnerships and grown our lead database from sixty to five thousand.

We made tens of thousands of sales in a couple of months, just by looking at how we could add value to complementary entities that also served our audience.

How Can You Position Yourself and Offer Value?

One of the most effective ways to generate quality prospects is through education.

You can educate your prospects on issues they may not even realize they're facing.

Start by showing them the implications of not making changes. By doing this, you can easily corner a market. That's how my company grew by more than 1,500 percent in three years.

First, create a special report. We called ours "The Seven Secrets of Top Producers." It consisted of interviews with members of our small client base, in which we asked them for their secrets to success.

Approach people in your industry — clients or not — and tell them you're putting together a report. You want to learn from their success. Ask them for their key habits or principles.

The psychology behind this is that everybody wants to know what the best performers in their field are doing.

By gathering and disseminating that information, you're automatically associated with the most successful people in the field. When you send out the report, invite other professionals — potential referral sources — to contribute a tactical lesson related to the report.

Now, you have supplementary material from people who have access to your ideal clients. And because you've included them, they're more like to help you distribute it to *their* clients.

Then, you can ask them if they're open to having some of their top clients interviewed for a similar series. You could do a webinar during which you interview their clients, and ask them to invite their audience.

When we did this, four hundred to six hundred people signed on to the webinar to hear a top producer in his field talk about our product. Can you see how much more effective this is than hearing *us* talk about our product?

And our sales team was busy for three weeks afterward.

The Takeaway

- ☐ Ask yourself what challenges your target market faces.

- ☐ Approach other professionals who serve your target market. Ask to interview some of their top clients for a special report.

- ☐ Ask the professionals to contribute, as well. Ask them to distribute the report to their audience.

- ☐ Create a series of webinars, blog posts, etc., in which you regularly feature top performers in your target industry. Ask your professional partners to invite their audience, as well.

CHAPTER 39

Top-Secret Website Tricks for Increasing Lead Conversions and Productivity

"The successful warrior is the average man, with laser-like focus."
—Bruce Lee

Application:
B2B,
B2C
Difficulty: Moderate
Time to implement: Two to three hours a week
Cost to implement: $50 to $100 a month for software

Shanah Kitzerow is the head of strategic marketing for Planning You Can Trust®. She's a sharp marketer who has logged seven years helping financial-services professionals build a marketing strategy, so she knows a thing or two about effective website marketing.

What I'd invite you to take away from this chapter is her simple checklist to ensure that each of her web pages converts at the highest possible rate. By ensuring that every page meets these guidelines, her firm was able to increase overall web traffic by a whopping 140 percent in six months!

And with more traffic going to an effective landing page, call volume went down by 40 percent. This freed up significant resources for other business development and sales activity.

Oh, and did I mention that conversions rose to 30 percent? Yup!

The Three-Point Checklist

Shanah has broken down her system into three smart questions.

#1: Do I have a consistently branded page for each marketing channel?

For each of your lines of business/target markets, make sure to have a designated landing page. The page should be branded and consistent with other material, such as brochures and e-mail messages.

Shanah recommends designing your landing page as a template that can be updated. That way, you can keep refreshing the page with new content (events, offers, etc.), which will help keep your search ranking high. She also recommends building in the ability to archive past events and offers — again, for SEO.

#2: Is my content relevant and my call to action clear?

Make sure the visitor knows what his next step is, and how to take it.

A call to action can be as simple as:

Complete this form to register for this event.

or

Complete this form to join our mailing list and learn about future events.

Make your forms concise, requiring only the most basic information: name, phone number, e-mail, how did you hear about us?

#3: Do I have a distinct added value or draw for my audience?

Directives such as, "View a video of our most recent event for a peek inside" or "Download our latest economic update to get a feel for what we will be covering" help promote and inform.

Notice how each of these actions is designed to take the visitor to a next step in his education. They are not sales pitches.

Some more tips from Shanah:

- Make sure your completed forms are tied back to Google Analytics. That way, you can track goal completion and conversions.
- Have the system send you an e-mail once a form is completed. Program it to identify in the subject line the marketing channel (i.e., landing page) from which the lead came.
- Triggered e-mail responses will definitely boost your success but they're not a must-have. You can get started without them by simply stating "Thank you for registering for our webinar."

- Use "Thank You" pages so that visitors know that their information went through.
- Your "Thank You" page should also clearly let prospects know exactly what to expect and when. Make your promises realistic, given your workflow: "You will receive a call within forty-eight hours of our event," for example, or "You will receive your complimentary certificate in the mail within the next seven to ten business days."

The Takeaway

Having a set checklist in place for your various marketing elements helps to drive consistency and conversions into your process. With all of the complexity you can encounter in digital marketing, it's a good idea to write down your processes.

Try this:

☐ Make a list of the steps you need to follow as you go about your next sales or marketing initiative.

☐ Invite someone in your agency to follow the steps and see if he can do it without your help.

☐ Keep refining the process until it can be done by anyone.

☐ Save the final, tested version as one of your standard operating procedures.

☐ Move on to the next process in your agency and duplicate.

CHAPTER 40

The Simple Yet Revealing Worksheet That Will Totally Transform the Way You Do Marketing

"If you aren't going all the way, why go at all?"
—Joe Namath

Application:
B2B,
B2C
Difficulty: Easy
Time to implement: Two hours
Cost to implement: Free

I'm sure you didn't become an insurance agent or financial advisor to spend all your time marketing and selling. You want to spend time with your clients — meeting new ones and strengthening your relationships with old ones.

But you see others marketing this way and that, and you think their strategies might work for you. Pretty soon, you are spending all your time marketing and barely any time with clients.

Instead, says Maria Marsala, you should be *managing* before *marketing*.

In this chapter, we're going to give you a simple but powerful tool to help you quickly determine UP FRONT whether you have a great client in front of you, or whether you should pass — regardless of how many assets under management he might have to add to your tally.

Stop "Spaghetti Marketing"

Maria is a consultative coach who works with agents to help them improve their processes and make more sales. She calls the typical advisor approach "spaghetti marketing," i.e., "throwing stuff up against the wall to see if it sticks. If it sticks, they'll try it out on a few other clients. But they really don't have a formal process in play."

Her point is that when you manage your marketing and sales before you start applying strategies, you can get a preview of what you're doing, how you'll do it, and how it will work. You'll be more effective. And ultimately, you'll have to do less of it.

The Simple Worksheet That Will Transform Your Business

Maria uses something called a Go/No-Go Sheet. Professionals in many other industries use these, too. In AEC (architecture, engineering, and construction), for example, people are bidding on huge proposals. Since they're vying for big jobs that net a lot of money, the proposals take a lot of time and cost a lot of money to write – up to $5,000! Before going through all of that, these professionals want to make sure the process is worth their time – that, if they got the job, it would be a good fit. So they assess the opportunity carefully before getting involved.

Most advisors don't think this way; they just dive in, willing to work with anybody who breathes, even if it's not a good fit.

The Go/No-Go Sheet lets you segment your target market. Then you can build a niche and serve them more effectively.

How does it work?

This matrix walks you through several steps:

1. Assess if you're currently niching.
2. Refine a niche.
3. Create an ideal client profile.
4. Segment your client base and "touches" for each segment.
5. Place the "guts" and insights from the process into a decision-making Go/No-Go matrix.
6. Use the Go/No-Go matrix to decide if a prospect is an ideal client for your firm.

The "prospect factors" you choose in the Go/No-Go Sheet are determined by the top characteristics of your ideal client. The "firm factors" you choose are determined by your mission, value statement, and vision.

Prospect Factors	Decision-Making Criteria		
	No - 1	Neutral - 3	Yes - 5
1 Prospect has sufficient knowledge of our firm to make a good decision about hiring us		3	
2 We are in front of the key decision-maker(s).	1		
3 Prospect has realistic expectations regarding our service level	1		
4 We have good rapport with prospect (Advisor/Team).			5
5 Prospect's AUM is in the range our firm prefers.		3	
6 Prospect is involved in the community.	1		
7 Pricing/fees are not the prospect's only deciding factor.			5
8 Prospect completes forms/communicates in a timely fashion.		3	
9 Prospect is technical enough to conduct virtual business.		3	
10 Prospect is highly committed & excited to create a plan.			5
SUBTOTAL - Prospect Information	3	12	15

Sample questions from a Go/No-Go Sheet.

For example:

- The prospect has already made a decision to move forward/make big changes.
- The prospect is a well-established executive or business owner with a growing company.
- There is no hesitation regarding doing business with us.
- The prospect understands the importance of making time for quarterly and yearly meetings.

A score is assigned to each statement. The goal is to get the prospect's score up to a certain level. If the score falls below that level, the prospect is a "No-Go." You don't want to do business with him, regardless of potential commissions.

If he scores within the "Go" range, you can engage for the sale.

Create a culture where anybody can make a sale.

Maria says that one of the most powerful things about a Go/No-Go Sheet is that it can be shared throughout your firm to get everybody on the same page.

One advisor filled out the matrix and put together an ideal-client profile as a result. And when he presented his findings to his staff, the office manager was able to put what he'd learned into practice and bring in a client. The office manager — not even an agent!

Get on the same page as your vendors and partners.

The worksheet is also a great document to give to anybody you hire to do your marketing, web design, or any other essential marketing and branding task.

It saves time at the outset by telling vendors and partners exactly whom you target. And it helps them get things right for you the first time around, saving more time and money.

Summary

Using a Go/No-Go Sheet can help you eliminate prospects who won't be a long-term fit for you. It helps to establish a standard in your agency that will predict success and which can be easily duplicated across all areas of your practice to help build consistency.

The Takeaway

☐ Create a list of the "must-have" elements you're looking for in a new client.

☐ Attribute a score to each quality, and create a threshold scale.

☐ Share the Sheet throughout your organization and with partners and vendors (marketing, web design, writing, etc.).

☐ Take it a step further and use the sheets to build profiles of ideal employees, vendors, etc.

CHAPTER 41

Reach More Business-to-Business Customers with White Papers

"Nothing is particularly hard if you divide it into small jobs."
—Henry Ford

Application: B2B
Difficulty: Moderate
Time to implement: One to four weeks
Cost to implement: $100 to $2,000

It's been my experience that the business that takes it upon itself to lead with education ends up with the lion's share of profits.

When I was starting out at a small startup, instead of trying to discount our way into sales, we developed really strong pieces of content that educated the market about how to grow their own businesses.

As a result, we grew quickly and organically, and built a substantial list of clients within a three-year time frame and hit the Inc. 5,000 list at #17 of all companies in the US. Our growth curve was astonishing: 1,503 percent in under three years!

What I learned was that the fastest way to grow your lead in the market is to **constantly create thought leadership and education to help your market rise above the confusion.** In the words of business-growth legend Jay Abraham, "People are silently begging to be led."

Ask yourself, who in your market is educating, leading, and showing clients the way to security, more profits, and/or peace of mind? Who is actively demonstrating that through thoughtful white papers, webinars, in-person events, blogging, e-mail messages, and the like?

In this chapter, I'm going to give you a step-by-step road map for gaining that market edge using content. It's one of the most overlooked pieces of authority-building you can use to separate yourself from the competition, generate leads, and get direct access to decision-makers in your market.

And if you know the "insider tricks," it can be very easy to do.

White Papers Versus Reports

I once had a client named Joseph, a commercial-lines producer looking for a way to get access to the elusive business market in his community. He had tried cold-calling, door-knocking, and attending early-morning networking meetings, but the going was tough.

Since he wasn't adding value to the market, I advised him to *SHIFT* his approach. I suggested that we start producing valuable pieces of content for the market as a way to attract the ideal prospects.

First off, we had to decide the kind of content we would produce. The most basic form is a PDF labeled either "white paper" or "special report."

A white paper is a special type of report that takes an elevated approach to a complex topic. It tends to be more professional and sophisticated than a special report. You can use the same strategy for coming up with content that I've laid out previously, but it should be aimed at a reader who is a bit more sophisticated.

I've found that calling these pieces "special reports" works best for converting consumers (senior products, health and life insurance, home and auto), but when dealing with the business-to-business community (commercial lines, group benefits, investments, etc.), it's best for conversion to call them "white papers."

If you don't want to write your white papers yourself, try to find writers experienced in writing specifically for the business community, as white papers require an expert voice. You can find many of these on Elance.com.

Finding Topics for Your White Paper

Joseph and I spent some time brainstorming topics related to what he sold by making a simple list of products, each of which could be the subject of a white paper:

- Commercial lines
- Group retirement products
- C-level compensation plans
- HR and benefit packages
- Defined contributions
- Self-funded plans

I know. They are pretty generic, right?

Then we headed over to Google and started crowdsourcing our content. What's "crowdsourcing"? It's a simple way to tap into a community to codevelop a project or piece of content, or find what's working already.

Using Google to see what others have written on a given topic and how you can adapt it is a great shortcut to content development, and a clever way to get your content written quickly. Just use what's already working!

Start by writing down your core area of focus, and then add keywords such as:

- Tips
- Ideas
- Report
- Study
- Survey

For example, Joseph was writing about annuities, so we did a Google search for "Annuity Tips" and "Annuity Study."

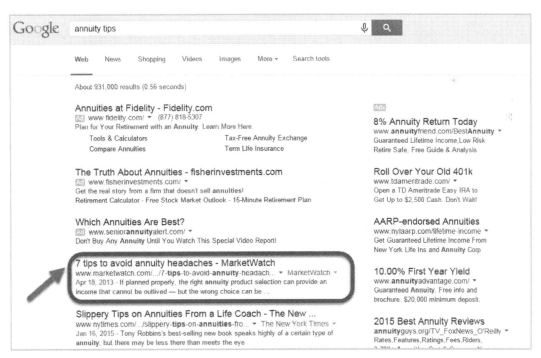

The number one result was a great article called "7 Tips to Avoid Annuity Headaches," written back in 2013 as a press release that made it onto MarketWatch.

Joseph then headed over fiverr.com and hired someone to do some "article spinning" for $5 to $10.

Be careful when doing this, though. You don't want your article written by a piece of software, so make sure your writer explicitly spells out that he will do the work by hand. And another thing: some articles don't allow you to rewrite them unless you have permission, so check to be sure you aren't violating someone's copyright.

To be clear, Joseph was not copying the article; that's outright plagiarism. What he was doing was having the story completely rewritten so it was a *brand-new* piece of content.

A Quick Aside on Press Releases

Let's take a quick break from talking about white papers for a minute to talk about press releases.

Did you notice the date on that article I picked? It's April 18, 2013. Years later, it's still ranking above the *New York Times!* How did they DO that? And how can you do the same?

It's a pretty simple formula actually, and may change a bit if Google updates its ranking algorithm between now and when you read this, but here are the basics:

Step 1: Write a press release in a story format, or have someone on elance.com do it for you for about $100 to $150.

Step 2: Pay a top-notch PR distribution company such as Business Wire to send it out for around $350.

> *Shameless Plug: If you're interested in Forbes, Entrepreneur, Mashable, BuzzFeed, and other such high-level outlets, please contact my office for details, as we have specialized services for advisors.*

Step 3: Go to fiverr.com and hire a contractor to do "SEO backlinks" for $5, and have them point the words "Annuity Tips" back to the most reputable website your press release was sent to.

This way, you'll have a release out on the major networks and some search-engine links that point back to the article.

Yes, it IS that simple!

OK, back to the main point . . .

Review Other Resources in Your City

Another idea Joseph and I pursued was to review various insurance programs and products available in his city.

Chances are, your clients don't know what their options are. You probably have access to carrier profiles and program requirements they've never seen before, because every agent before you has shown them only "good fits."

Clients want as much information as possible at the beginning of the buying process. Create a simple white paper that includes the name of your city. For example: "Chicago Commercial Insurance Programs: Reviewed and Rated."

And since you are the person reviewing and rating them, you can contribute your expert voice, which will help bolster your credibility.

Or, here's another idea: "Denver Benefit Advisors: Reviewed and Assessed."

Here, you can use your experience to point out the weaknesses of other advisors.

Offer the white paper to local HR managers via LinkedIn, or post it in local groups as a "service to the community."

Once Joseph had completed his white paper we reached out to local firms that were potential power partners for him — in his case, attorneys, CPAs, and business consulting firms. He invited them to contribute a page to the white paper, offering them full credit.

He then sent this more well-rounded report to his internal e-mail database of twelve hundred contacts (including his LinkedIn contacts). His partners were pleased to have the report distributed to their contacts as well, so he added another eight hundred people to his database from their lists. When recipients attempted to download the white paper, they were prompted to enter their contact information.

By the end of the month, Joseph had an inbox full of prospects and back-to-back appointments lined up for sales opportunities. Incredible!

Summary

Creating thought leadership pieces can be a powerful way to gain market credibility, generate leads, and gain market advantage. Though writing them yourself can be tough, using content that's already popular can shave hours off of your decision-making process.

Google can be a great resource for compiling and crowd-sourcing your ideas. Using outsourced writers from online networks can further shortcut your speed to market. Inviting partners to collaborate on your piece can double or triple your exposure base and open up a new source of leads you hadn't had access to before.

What piece of content did this chapter inspire you to come up with? What could you Google right now to start generating ideas for the title of your report?

The Takeaway

☐ Brainstorm challenges and risks your business customers face.

☐ Use Google to come up with content ideas.

☐ Use your experience and expertise to guide the white paper content.

☐ Hire a writer to build the white paper or "spin" the content.

☐ Distribute the finished white paper via LinkedIn or other social networks.

CONCLUSION

We've covered how to get your name out there. You know how to look your best, speak your best, and broadcast your best far and wide.

Now, it's time to start closing sales.

In our next book, *The Second SHIFT: Sales Strategies for a New Era,* we'll cover the most effective, highest-grossing techniques from the world's top insurance agents, brokers, and financial advisors.

Here's a sneak peek at what you can expect from *The Second SHIFT.*

The Brilliant $3,000 Door-Opening Sales Strategy and Closer That One of My Students Taught Me

"If we all did the things we are capable of doing,
we would literally astound ourselves."
—Thomas Edison

This *SHIFT* comes courtesy of one of my clients, Michael B.

It has to do with the way you approach a potential client or business partner.

Michael is a hardworking, successful benefits broker out of Cincinnati. He developed an incredibly creative strategy for getting in front of business owners with fifty or more employees.

Bolstering Benefits with Free Gifts

Michael's target market was businesses that couldn't afford benefits, to whom he could then offer individual plans through a private exchange.

He put together a package that included discounts to a local amusement park, the Cincinnati Zoo, LA Fitness, and other national brands, as well as banking benefits and free sessions with a financial educator.

It took him about a year to build his package. When all was said and done, he could offer more than $2,000 worth of rebates, coupons, discounts, and free samples from notable businesses.

He would then reach out to local businesses and offer this package to them to give to their employees. This got him in the door almost immediately.

How He Got His Foot in the Door

Here's how Michael first contacted business owners.

His pitch was pretty simple:

> *Hi. My name is Michael. I help businesses without health-insurance plans provide valuable health benefits to the employees cost-free, and I'd like to take twenty minutes of your time in person. And, as a thank-you, even if you don't decide to do business with me, I would like to give $1,000 worth of coupons from local businesses to each one of your employees — as a gift from you. I'll stay completely out of it, and I don't expect any credit for it. All I want is twenty minutes of your time. At the very least, you'll walk away with the gratitude of your employees for the $1,000-worth of coupons YOU will give each and every one of them.*

Bingo, Michael got that appointment — and delivered that $1,000-worth of value to each employee.

Then, he sweetened the pot even further:

> *So that's my presentation. If you decide to do this with me and allow me to talk to all of your employees about health insurance, I will triple the value of those coupons and give you all the other valuable discounts that I have, which amounts to about $3,000 per person.*

This wasn't just a door opener. It was a closer.

All Michael did was use some of the coupons to get in the door and the rest to close it.

In the space of one year, Michael was able to present his concept to eighteen hundred employees in direct, one-on-one meetings. He's spoken to groups as large as two hundred to explain the free benefits that their employers had negotiated.

His process was straightforward.

He had two agents call businesses to schedule a free presentation to their employees.

In some instances, he had a financial educator — who offered a discount as part of the package — make the presentation. Then, Michael got up and discussed the benefits that employees could purchase.

He was even able to partner with a local bank that offered $50 dollars to anybody who enrolled within seven days of the meeting.

Naturally, the employees were thrilled.

This approach helped Michael in two key ways.

Eliminating the Business Owners' Objection

First, it completely eliminated the objection by business owners who said, "We already have someone we work with for benefits."

Keep in mind that this was before the Affordable Care Act. But you could use it today for smaller groups that reply, "We can't afford benefits and neither can our employees."

When faced with this objection, Michael would respond, "Hey, I know how you feel, and that's why we put this together."

Offering Value Independent of a Sale

With the inclusion of all of those coupons, rebates, and samples, everybody got something. Whether they could afford benefits or not, they didn't walk away empty-handed.

Everyone received something of value from the presentation.

The Results of Michael's Hard Work

After his presentation, Michael would sit down one-on-one with each of the employees to show them how they could get the benefits he'd described.

Inevitably, even though the employer had gone in thinking that none of his people could afford it, Michael signed up a group of people after every meeting.

Here are two additional revenue streams I was able to help Michael take advantage of, flowing from this one strategy.

Bonus Revenue Stream #1

Let's say he met with two thousand people every year and 10 percent of them took advantage of a Life Time Fitness membership that was part of the package.

The value of that membership to Life Time Fitness is around $500.

Michael could easily negotiate a small finder's fee for each one of the people who signed up.

That could be worth tens of thousands of dollars.

Bonus Revenue Stream #2

When I shared Michael's strategy with a small mastermind group, half the people in the benefits business wanted it.

And they were willing to pay him for it.

So he was able to start looking at his program as a franchise-type model that he could license to noncompeting advisors.

Michael got three revenue streams out of one little *SHIFT:* by introducing the value he could provide to employees with health insurance, instead of presenting himself as a health-insurance or benefits consultant.

The Takeaway

- ☐ Contact local businesses and put together a small package of offers you can use to open the door to your ideal prospects.
- ☐ Focus on your target market's key objections.
- ☐ Offer value designed to eliminate their objections and open the door to a conversation.

My Ultra-Special Gift for Amazon Reviewers

You made it! Allow me to extend my hand in a virtual handshake to truly congratulate you on making it through this first book!

You can smile knowing that we've officially reached the end of the book.

As a reward, I have a special bonus for you that will take your prospecting efforts to the next level — if you can do me a small favor.

Before I give it to you, I'm going to try and persuade you to comply with my request — really, my heartfelt plea.

I need you to purchase one hundred copies of this book to give to your fellow advisors and agents so we can help spread the industry *SHIFT*.

I'm kidding!

The favor is pretty small, actually.

If, and ONLY if, you thought the information in this book was valuable, thought-provoking, and/or helpful, could you write a positive review on Amazon? (I'm gunning for five stars!)

This would help me out tremendously, and also help all of us promote an industry *SHIFT* by spreading the knowledge far and wide.

Once you've created and posted your review, send it in an e-mail to coach@ agencygrowthacademy.com, including the username you used on Amazon.

Within twenty-four to forty-eight hours, my staff will review it and send you an incredible bonus gift that outlines my exclusive S.A.S. Technique, step by step. This strategy has generated applause from industry insiders and is a very stealthy way to accomplish three important marketing objectives:

- Build top-level partnerships;
- Get deep insider data on your prospects; and
- Generate the highest-quality leads.

I only teach S.A.S. to my high-level masterminds, but I'm willing to give it to you if you would do me the small honor of leaving me a review right now.

Finally, if you want to stay in touch, subscribe to my weekly updates at www. agencygrowthacademy.com, where I share more strategies for using the *SHIFT* to market and sell more policies, AUM, and retirement planning.

The True Goal of *SHIFT*

So, there you have it.

I've provided you with all of the best *SHIFT*s you can make to take your business to the next level.

Now that I've these successful methodologies, you might wonder why I wrote this book.

Why would I give away something worth billions of dollars of premiums sold and hundreds of millions in commissions?

Wisdom that's taken decades to develop?

Ideas from the brightest minds in the industry?

I'll be frank: a lot of people told me I shouldn't do this.

A lot of folks thought I should just keep these ideas to myself, grow my consulting practice, and profit from the content in this book for many years to come. FMOs approached me to teach their agents my systems and pay me a back-end fee.

But, having gone through this book, you might have noticed that immediate and long-term profit don't really juice me.

Why Profit Isn't as Important as You Might Think

I've had the chance to live in some incredible parts of the world, and on my journeys, I've been told that my wife and I touched the lives of other people on a personal level.

My wife and I have dedicated ourselves to improving the lives of others. We've worked with abused kids, recovering heroin addicts, and orphans and refugees from Colombia, Africa, and Haiti.

We've had our fair share of life-changing encounters, and these have made us appreciate what life is really about.

When you look into the eyes of people who have faced tremendous pain, you know you want your life to be about more than helping your own business grow.

How We Can Change the World, One Client at a Time

Of course, I'm not naïve. I understand that this book will have a significant financial impact on my business. It will create a lot of demand for my private consulting, my training programs, our Done for You services, and seminars.

In fact, I've attracted a lot of business just from *mentioning* this book.

But my goal for *SHIFT* is a lot larger. In fact, it's something so ambitious that its impossibility almost frightens me.

You see, I want *SHIFT* to serve as a wake-up call to one of the most important industries in the world.

With this book, every advisor and agent on Earth has access to the tools they need to truly serve their community.

Even if each of you serves only one person by employing the principles in this book, that's *one more person* who will have peace of mind.

Multiply that times the millions of insurance agents and financial advisors all over the world, and we could bring peace of mind and security to millions of people.

And that is my big, hairy, audacious goal.

Join Me in the *SHIFT* Movement

Do I think this can be done? Absolutely. But I can't do it by myself.

I'm so thrilled and humbled that you and I connected, that you are now part of this movement: the *SHIFT* Movement.

It's one of those rare opportunities that takes by storm an industry where people can connect, collaborate, and transform an entire state, country, and — yes — even the world.

If we can change the way we help people with their health, their life, their retirement, their goals for the future, the fruits of their years of hard work and savings, then you and I can change the face of the planet.

I haven't held anything back.

This is the part I play: Creating this movement and pushing it forward.

I sincerely hope that you will apply the principles you read here.

I hope that you will refine them and even make them better so that *SHIFT* can grow and take on a momentum all its own.

Let's talk about how to do that. Let's talk about where you and I can go from here.

Head over to www.Theshiftnation.org to learn about how we might work together.

Step One: Become a Member of *SHIFT* Nation

There's an African proverb that says, "If you want to go quickly, go alone. If you want to go farther, go together."

Based on this ideal, we have created a membership program to bring together like-minded insurance agents and financial advisors to share fresh and innovative ideas around marketing, sales, business growth and mindset.

We do this through incredible new strategies, compelling interviews with top producers, group masterminds, new ideas, as well as new tips and techniques working in the field right now every month.

It's also the best way to get a first look at the new techniques that are *SHIFT*ing the industry today!

All for one low monthly fee.

Enroll today and get a special gift at www.TheShiftNation.org

Step Two: Become a Nationally Cited Authority in Insurance or Financial Services

I've paid over half a million dollars to public-relations firms in hopes of getting my clients and I in the media. PR firms made a lot of promises to get us on different outlets, yet in most cases, they could just never get the job done — and hardly any will guarantee results.

So I went out and started our own boutique PR firm that GUARANTEES insurance agents and advisors get media exposure so they can have that incredible branding and credibility that goes with being able to say "As seen on . . .".

Advisors have told us their clients are taking them more seriously, they close faster and seminar attendance has gone up by 128 percent by using this in their marketing.

We have gotten over two hundred professionals on digital outlets like CNN, Forbes, Fortune, Inc., MSNBC, CNBC, and TV programs such as *After the Bell, Fox Business News, Closing Bell, Bloomberg, Squawk Box, The Rachael Ray Show, Steve Harvey*, and many more.

All guaranteed, or you don't pay a dime.

Learn more at www.GuaranteedMediaServices.com.

Step Three: Let Me Do the Work for You

If you would like my team to actually do some of the prospecting for you, specifically on LinkedIn — using all my insider techniques, strategies, and e-mail templates — we can do that for you.

Head over to www.YourInstantAuthority.com to see the testimonials and learn about the process, then set up a strategy call.

Step Four: Platinum Partnership — Invitation Only

My Platinum Partnership program allows producers, advisors, and agents who are already successful to take their success to a whole new level. It's an intimate, one-on-one relationship that includes biweekly mentoring sessions, high-level mastermind meetings with like-minded advisors laser-focused on growth. This program is not for everyone, as I can only work with so many people at this level.

We currently have an NFL celebrity turned advisor, Million Dollar Round Table members, published authors, wealth advisors, group-benefits advisors, life producers, a private-placement expert who works exclusively with accredited investors, and many more.

Among the achievements of our members: doubling the closing ratio at group seminars, reducing their cost per acquisition by 500 percent, generating over forty leads of HR directors at Silicon Valley's richest companies in under twenty days, and selling untold millions in premium in record time.

Please note that this is a comprehensive program that requires a minimum five-figure investment in exchange for six-figure returns.

If you would like to be invited to apply, please visit www.Theshiftnation.org.

Acknowledgements

There's a proverb that says "It takes a village to raise a child". It's also true that "It takes a village to create a book". To that end, I'd like to thank the following people who have been instrumental in the creating of this book and the wisdom found within it.

First, my best friend, confidant, coach, psychologist, cheerleader and wife: Anaïse. You are the light of my life. Without your patience, encouragement and support this book would not be possible. I can't wait to see what our life adventures bring us next. Mom and Dad: a guy could not ask for more loving, supporting and caring parents. You raised me right with the best you had and taught me how to lead "the real life". Though we never had much materially, our life was rich beyond compare. I love you. To my brother, Mathew, no one else can make me laugh like a little kid. Thank you for keeping me humble. Luc, your wisdom has helped me see things I couldn't has been invaluable. Anne, thank you for being my 'second set of eyes' and avoiding what could have been a disastrous first book!

To my editor, Christina Lembo, thank you for making my words come to life and helping good words become even better! Rally, thank you for all you've done to support this project through all the interviews and late night rushes.

To Clint Jones and Brandon Cruz, you guys gave me my first introduction to this incredible industry and took a chance on a young Canadian transplant when no one else would. The lessons I've learned from the whirlwind growth days are better than any Ivy League education I could buy. Your entrepreneurial spirit and willingness to test and learn were the foundation of my learning. Sully, Mahoney, Shane - there couldn't have been a better group of guys to grow and succeed with than you. It's a gift to have worked beside each of you and learned from you.

Jay Abraham, your words inside 'Your Secret Wealth' opened up a world of possibility and adventure I never dreamed possible. Your years of teaching, resources, mentorship and friendship have been exceedingly generous and more than I could have ever expected. Thank you for giving me a PhD in marketing, strategy and preeminence. Your words are not wasted.

Tony Robbins, from the early days of Personal Power to Awaken the Giant Within to the privilege being on stage with you in Milwaukee - each moment has taught me how to 'Step up!' and live my life in service of others. I've learned so much from your mastery of communication and how to generate peak states within myself, I can't thank you enough.

Alex Mandossian, you have been a trusted ally and sage when it came to deciding what direction this book would go. When I retreated to the mountains to write this book, that one call we had shaped the entire future that has now become the reality of this book. Big hug, brother!

Michael Levin, for our stimulating conversations and expert advice that helped bring this book to fruition. Your blend of honesty, encouragement and wisdom has made this book what it is today. Frankly, this book may never have made the light of day without your note that this manuscript needed to be shared with the world. It was THE turning point I needed. Forever grateful.

Martin Carr, you gave me my first crack at the world of writing when you accepted my early writing under 'Web Gorilla'. This book is indeed an evolution of those days! Thank you for your friendship, collaboration and support.

Jim Kellner, you believed in me and backed up (almost) every out-of-the-box idea I had to bring Applied to the next level. Your warm, humble and down-to-earth leadership style has taught me mountains on how to lead your organization by being a servant. I will cherish our times together. Reid French, for introducing me to a new paradigm of thought on how to plan for organizational expansion. Ian Hoffman, whose direction opened a new door of possibility I would have never expected. I'm grateful for you!

Danette A.K.A 'Dee' - my life would be a jumbled chaos without your steely nerves and 'up all night' support through all our entrepreneurial adventures. You are brilliant and beautiful. Thank you for keeping the ship together! Leigh and Nicole, your 'conquer all' attitude and indomitable spirit are the beating heart of our programs.

David Callanan, your vision and desire to serve coupled with rare humility in the face of enormous success are what we need more of in the world of business. Thank you for your friendship and partnership. You are an example to us all. Keep shining.

So many others are deserving of thanks for their help, support and leadership in and outside the insurance and financial space including Don Brailsford, Alan Katz, Paul Feldman, Josh Hilgers, Janet Trautwein, James Leitner, Sam Melamed, Eben Pagan, Jeff Walker, Joe Jablonski, Mike Filsaime, Scott Lingle, Chip Bacciocco, Amy McIlwain, Scott Cantrell, Nelson Griswold, Walt Podgurski, Steve Anderson, Randy Schwantz, Joe Simonds, Jovan Will, Fernando Godinez, Brad Petersen, Bond Halpert, Ted McGrath, Bill Daniel, Bill Cates, Bob Burg, Brandon Stuerke, Cal Durland, Dennis McGough, Dan Mangus, Dan Sullivan, Dan Vinal, Deborah Sternberg, Gordon Quentin, Jennifer Grazel, Jennifer Grazel, Joe Stevens, John Kurath, Lynne Wallace, Maria Marsala, Matt

Anderson, Michael Kitces, Steve Savant, Susan Combs, Tom Carolan, Travis Lee, Troy Wilson, Walk Gdowski, Marc Wheeler, Josh Turner, Matt Kistler, Matt Pardine, Michelle Abraham, Rob Mosquera, Rob Liano, Adam Maggio, Tom Hegna, Latesha Burroughs, Mark Rosenthal, Dr. Billy Williams, Seth Greene, Ken McArthur and Mark Seghers. You all help keep raising the bar of knowledge and insight in the industry to helps us make that *SHIFT*.

If I have omitted you for any reason, forgive me - you know who you are!

Made in the USA
Charleston, SC
10 March 2017